WHEELER BASIN LIBRARY
3 1564 00441 8057
W9-BZC-192

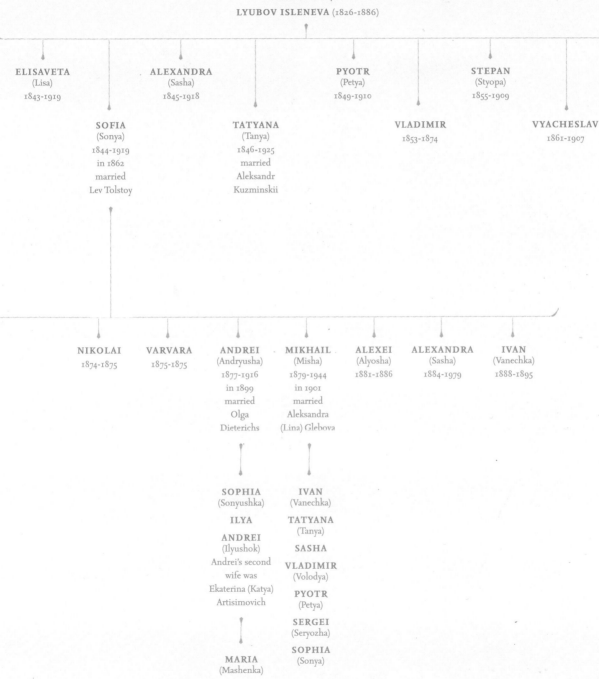

ANDREI BEHRS (1808-1868)
married in 1842
LYUBOV ISLENEVA (1826-1886)

- **ELISAVETA** (Lisa) 1843-1919
- **SOFIA** (Sonya) 1844-1919, in 1862 married Lev Tolstoy
  - **NIKOLAI** 1874-1875
  - **VARVARA** 1875-1875
  - **ANDREI** (Andryusha) 1877-1916, in 1899 married Olga Dieterichs
    - **SOPHIA** (Sonyushka)
    - **ILYA**
    - **ANDREI** (Ilyushok)
    - Andrei's second wife was Ekaterina (Katya) Artisimovich
      - **MARIA** (Mashenka)
  - **MIKHAIL** (Misha) 1879-1944, in 1901 married Aleksandra (Lina) Glebova
    - **IVAN** (Vanechka)
    - **TATYANA** (Tanya)
    - **SASHA**
    - **VLADIMIR** (Volodya)
    - **PYOTR** (Petya)
    - **SERGEI** (Seryozha)
    - **SOPHIA** (Sonya)
  - **ALEXEI** (Alyosha) 1881-1886
  - **ALEXANDRA** (Sasha) 1884-1979
  - **IVAN** (Vanechka) 1888-1895
- **ALEXANDRA** (Sasha) 1845-1918
- **TATYANA** (Tanya) 1846-1925, married Aleksandr Kuzminskii
- **PYOTR** (Petya) 1849-1910
- **VLADIMIR** 1853-1874
- **STEPAN** (Styopa) 1855-1909
- **VYACHESLAV** 1861-1907

Decatur Public Library
504 Cherry Street NE
Decatur, AL 35601

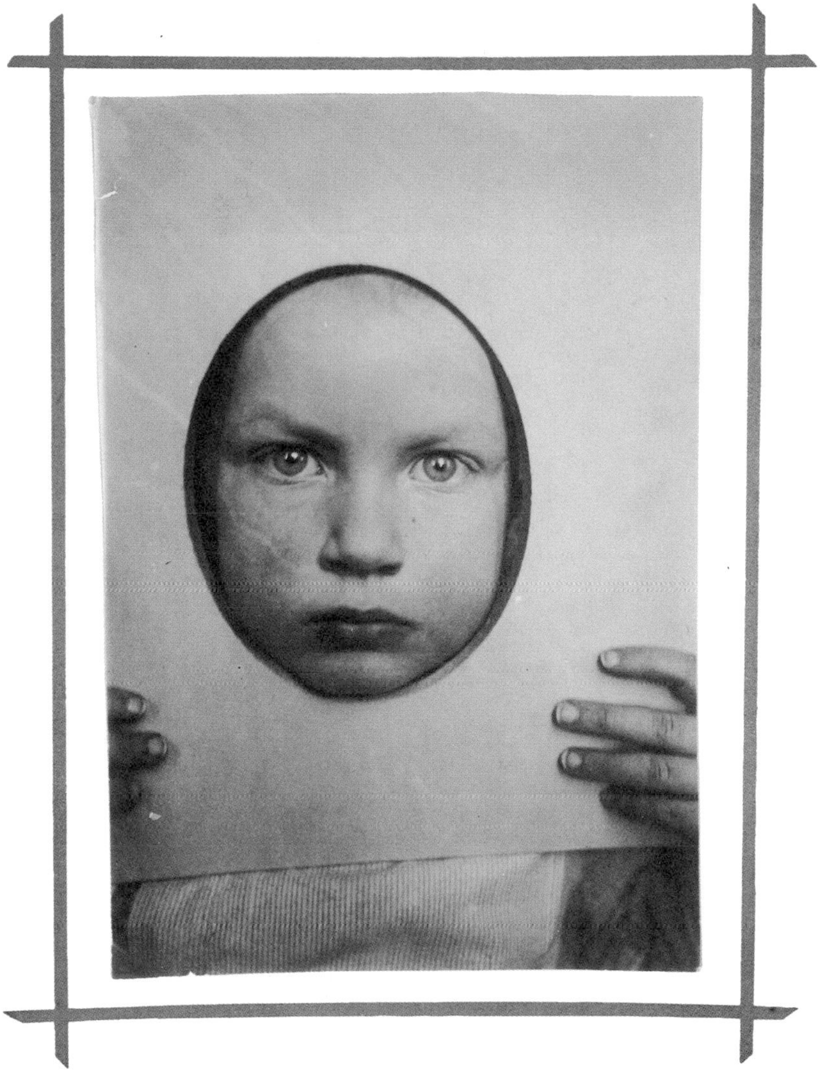

SOPHIA TOLSTOY'S KODAK CAMERA AND 13 BY 18 CM. GLASS PLATES

B 919.072
Tolstoy

Song Without Words

The Photographs & Diaries of Countess Sophia Tolstoy

LEAH BENDAVID-VAL

NATIONAL GEOGRAPHIC
WASHINGTON, D.C.

Decatur Public Library
504 Cherry Street NE
Decatur, AL 35601

"COUNTESS SOPHIA TOLSTOY IS WRITING THE HISTORY OF HER LIFE," YASNAYA POLYANA, 1906

Contents

Special thanks to:

Vitaly Remizov, Director
STATE MUSEUM OF L. N. TOLSTOY
MOSCOW

Marina Loginova, Head of Photographic Collections Division
STATE MUSEUM OF L. N. TOLSTOY
MOSCOW

Natalia Kalinina, Deputy Director, Records and Documents
STATE MUSEUM OF L. N. TOLSTOY
MOSCOW

Yuri Koudinov, Deputy Director, International Relations
STATE MUSEUM OF L. N. TOLSTOY
MOSCOW

Vladimir Tolstoy, Director
STATE MUSEUM OF L. N. TOLSTOY
AT YASNAYA POLYANA

Galina Alexeeva,
Head of Academic Research Department
STATE MUSEUM OF L. N. TOLSTOY
AT YASNAYA POLYANA

Andrei Baskakov, President
RUSSIAN UNION OF ART PHOTOGRAPHERS

Nikolai Romanov,
Researcher and Russian Translator

Foreword

Vladimir Tolstoy

SOPHIA ANDREYEVNA TOLSTAYA (TOLSTOY)—hers was a life lived on a grand scale, rich in substance, tragic, yet at the same time happy.

Forget about the great Lev for a moment and think of the fate of the woman who gave the world 13 Tolstoy children—among them Sergei, Tatyana, Ilya, Lev, Mikhail, and Alexandra—real personalities one and all. Think of the anguish of the mother who stoically bore the loss of five of her babies—Varenka, Nikolenka, Petya, Alyosha, and the family's darling, angelic Vanechka—and then, adding to her pain, the loss of two more children, Maria and Andrei, already grown into productive adults. Think of the grandmother, who lived to the see the birth of 31 grandchildren and one great-grandchild.

Isn't that enough for any single lifetime?

Like her husband, Sophia Andreyevna devoted her life to serving people. Her destiny was not to serve all humanity, but instead to devote herself to those people who were close to her, who were in need of daily care, warmth, and tenderness.

Sophia Andreyevna was a human being who undertook much and succeeded a great deal by any measure. To quote the poet and family friend Afanasy Fet, she was always "busy as a bee." In addition to her widely known feat of copying Lev Nikolaevich's manuscripts—arduous and consequential to say the least—she was a personality in her own right, a talent who left the world hundreds of unique and accomplished photographs made by her own hand.

She maintained and protected the family estate, Yasnaya Polyana—and in fact went beyond that. During the lifetime of Lev Tolstoy she created a comfortable home and provided a beautiful domestic haven for her family, and then later she preserved the house as a museum, a living monument to the genius after his death.

Isn't that enough for any single lifetime?

Yet she had still additional enthusiasms—for painting, music, philosophy, and her own literary efforts.

But the main thing for her was love—a love of enormous force: passionate, tormented by jealousy and by incessant doubt, a nervous love bordering on madness—but love, still love and nothing else!

Dearest Sophia Andreyevna! Let them argue and debate about whether you were the "evil genius" behind the great Lev. For him you were a worthy Lioness, a faithful wife, a loving mother of his children, and a tender, caring grandmother for his grandchildren. Now, today, with the passage of almost 163 years since your birth and 88 years since your death, there are Tolstoys living throughout the wide world, and in Russia, and in Yasnaya Polyana.

Doesn't that merit our gratitude?

We bow to you with deepest respect.

Vladimir Tolstoy

YASNAYA POLYANA

SELF-PORTRAIT IN THE KLINY ALLÉE, YASNAYA POLYANA, 1903

Introduction

Sonya's Themes

THE PHOTOGRAPH ON THE FACING PAGE—a self-portrait—is of Countess Sophia Andreyevna Tolstoy, wife of Lev Tolstoy, author of *Anna Karenina* and *War and Peace*. Sophia made the picture after she had been married 31 years.

She had fallen madly in love with Tolstoy in 1862, when she was a girl of 18. He was 34 and known in Russia as a promising author. Charismatic and attractive , he had women to choose from. Young Sophia Behrs, the second daughter in a household Tolstoy had frequented for years, was not the most obvious choice. Sophia's sister Lisa, older and by tradition the first in line for marriage, was a more likely candidate. Tolstoy had considered Lisa, but he eventually chose Sophia who was high-spirited and full of heart. On September 16, 1862, to the astonishment of the Behrs family, Tolstoy proposed. The news was particularly unwelcome to Lisa. Dr. Andrey Behrs, the girls' father, gave permission only reluctantly. The two sisters never quite got over it. Only a week after Tolstoy's proposal, on September 23, 1862, the couple was married in Moscow in an opulent ceremony at the Church of the Nativity of the Blessed Virgin. The new Countess Tolstoy, shy and a little afraid, began her wedded life.

On the pages of this book she is called Sonya, the informal name used by her family and friends and in letters and diaries. This version of her name matches the domestic mood, content, and viewpoint of her pictures. Diaries and letters—Sonya's, her husband's, sister's, and children's—reflect, support, and enlarge Sonya's photographic viewpoints. Taken together the pictures and words portray the full complexity of Sonya's personality, and tell her story.

During the course of a long, tumultuous, often painful marriage, Sonya engaged in a range of pursuits, practical and impractical, always with boundless energy. She photographed as she did everything else—with immense enthusiasm. And she had a strong instinct for composition.

By the time she made this picture she had already produced dozens of self-portraits, some romantic like this one and others more intimate. She photographed almost everybody and everything around her. Sonya believed her husband was a genius from the first days of their marriage, maybe earlier, and she made many of her photographs of him and their life together with posterity in mind.

Like everyone else, she saw the world through a filter of memory. Memories—fragmentary, layered, and imperfect—define who we are to ourselves and to everybody else. History is memory made official, supported by documents where possible—

but whose? In Sonya's photographs and written diaries she set out to generate an accurate, enduring record about herself, her husband, and her family that would one day be her legacy: She would bequeath to the world a full, in-depth Tolstoy family history. What future generations thought mattered to her.

But in her photography she went beyond the mere collecting of data. She enjoyed photography, taking pictures of people she liked being with, giving the trophies as gifts. And she worked very hard at her pictures. She made photographs and kept a diary because she felt impelled to document her introspections and to satisfy some undefined need in herself.

Sonya first took up photography in 1860, the summer she was 16. Photography was brand new and cumbersome at the time. Sonya was introduced to it by an acquaintance of her father's, a student known as Kukuly, who taught her to use his camera, then gave it to her as a gift. "I was enthusiastic about photography the whole summer," she said in her never-published autobiography, but at the end of that summer she dropped it and took up writing. None of those summer portraits of family and friends survived.

More than 25 years passed before she turned her attention to photography again. Beginning in 1887 she gradually spent more and more time at it, eventually producing most of her pictures between 1895 and 1910. But photography never became a full-time occupation, and her work remained unknown to a wider world. In part this is because Lev Tolstoy held the then nearly universal belief that a woman's role was to cater full-time to her husband and family. In daily life Sonya railed against this view while she paradoxically embraced it: She always remained completely in the shadow of her famous husband.

She was in awe of and in love with Lev Tolstoy for 48 years. For half that time she struggled against his social and religious principles; through all of it she helped him with his literary work as best she could and took care of his every physical need. To say she was prodigiously energetic is an understatement: She managed a complicated life that included having 13 children (eight lived to adulthood), handling the practical intricacies of estate business, and undertaking personal creative enterprises into which she poured her strong feelings and refined tastes. The Tolstoy marriage was stormy and ended badly, in part because Sonya was emotional and jealous. (Her husband had these same traits.) She was often unhappy and exhausted, but despite this she saw beauty around her and she put it into her photography.

This book, Sonya's story, is organized around the themes she photographed—her self-portraits, pictures of her husband, family scenes, the household staff and local peasantry, the artists, musicians, and writers who were her houseguests, the great family estate itself, and then back to Lev—the annual wedding anniversary photography sessions and, finally, sickness and death.

Her desire to make history backfired. Historians maligned her in part because of her increasingly bad behavior later in life, but mostly because she didn't accept the philosophy of her revered husband. But history is constantly rewritten, and so she has another chance.

She matters to us now not only for what she left behind (her photographic legacy is significant) but also because her longings—to have a life filled with creativity, purpose, and love—mirror desires we all have. She led the life of a 19th century Russian aristocrat but her endless effort to balance conflicting demands and possibilities is recognizable to us today, in some ways remarkably so. ■

SELF-PORTRAIT WITH LILIES ON WHITSUNDAY, GASPRA, CRIMEA, MAY 1902

LEV TOLSTOY, GASPRA, CRIMEA, OCTOBER 1901

LEV TOLSTOY, YASNAYA POLYANA, 1906

SELF-PORTRAIT SITTING FOR PAINTER YULIA IGUMNOVA, YASNAYA POLYANA, OCTOBER 11, 1899

4418057 7/08

SELF-PORTRAIT WITH DAUGHTER SASHA AND DAUGHTER-IN-LAW SONYA, KHAMOVNIKI, MOSCOW, 1895

Decatur Public Library
504 Cherry Street NE
Decatur, AL 35601

DAUGHTER-IN-LAW DORA AND HER CHILDREN WITH HOUSEKEEPER MAKING JAM, YASNAYA POLYANA, JUNE 1900

THE VILLAGE OF YASNAYA POLYANA, 1896

SON ILYA WITH HIS CHILDREN MIKHAIL, ANDREI, AND ILYA, MANSUROVO ESTATE, KALUGA PROVINCE, CIRCA 1905

MIKHAIL, ANDREI, AND ILYA TOLSTOY, CIRCA 1900

THE MIDDLE POND WITH BATHHOUSE, YASNAYA POLYANA, 1897

SELF-PORTRAIT WITH DAUGHTER SASHA IN ARBOR TOWER IN THE LOWER PARK, YASNAYA POLYANA, 1896

LEV TOLSTOY WITH INJURED LEG, YASNAYA POLYANA, 1908

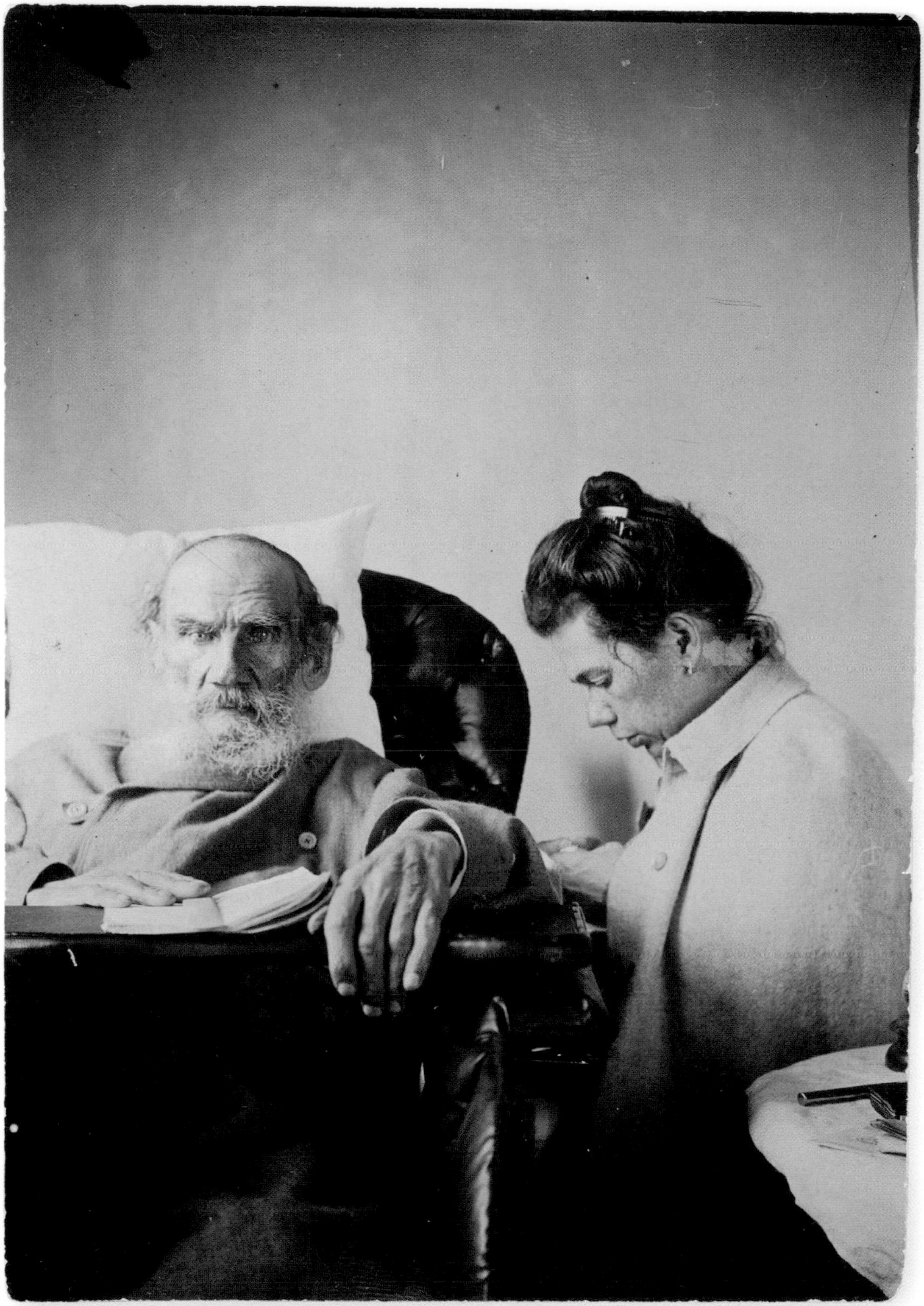

LEV TOLSTOY WITH DAUGHTER TANYA, GASPRA, CRIMEA, 1902

SELF-PORTRAIT WITH GRANDDAUGHTER TANYA, YASNAYA POLYANA, 1906

LEV TOLSTOY AND JAPANESE WRITER TOKUTOMY ROKA, WITH DAUGHTER SASHA ON BOX, JUNE 18, 1906

(following pages) SONYA'S DIARY **14 July 1897**
I have been developing photographs all day, and making prints of the ones people have asked for.... Here is a picture of me, cut out of an unsuccessful group with Tanya. People say I actually look much younger, probably because I have a high color. We walked to the river for a swim. There was a north wind and the sky was clear. I was exhausted all evening. Lev Nikolaevich invited me out for a walk, and I was delighted to accept. Misha started talking to me today with unwonted frankness and passion about his tormenting sexual urges, which are making him feel quite ill; he longed to remain pure, he said, but feared that he would succumb. My poor boys! They have no father, and what advice can I possibly give them in these matters? I know nothing of this side of a man's life. Tanya went to Tula today. Lev Nikolaevich is in high spirits; he was telling me all about his cycle ride to Tula to attend a meeting of the cycle club, where they discussed races and various other bicycle matters. Yet another interest of his! I feel so apathetic. I wrote Lyova, replied to various business letters, paid the wages, did the accounts and copied out more of Lev Nikolaevich's article "On Life" for him. I try to be cheerful and keep feverishly busy. I was copying for Lev Nikolaevich until 3 in the morning. (Note under photograph: "I am 53.")

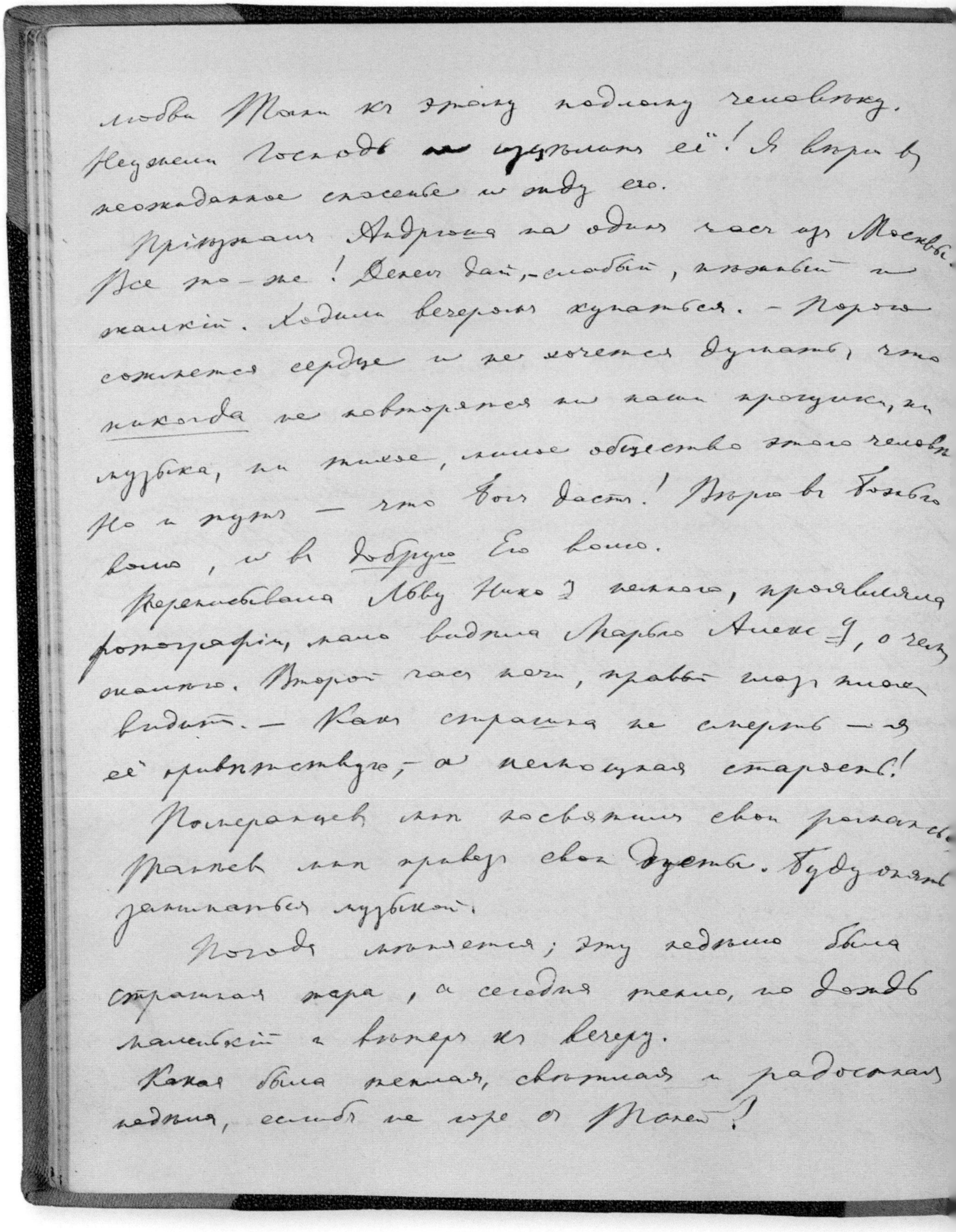

любви Тани къ этому подлому человѣку. Неужели Господь не спасетъ её! Я вѣрю въ неожиданное спасенiе и чудо его.

Прiѣзжалъ Андрюша на одинъ часъ изъ Москвы. Все то-же! Денегъ дай, — слабый, лживый и жалкiй. Ходили вечеромъ купаться. — Порой сожмется сердце и не хочется думать, что никогда не повторятся ни наши прогулки, ни музыка, ни тихое, милое общество этого человѣка. Но и пусть — что Богъ дастъ! Вѣрю въ Божью волю, и въ добрую Его волю.

Переписывала Льву Никол. немного, проявляла фотографiи, мало видѣла Марью Алекс., о чемъ жалѣю. Второй часъ ночи, правый глазъ плохо видитъ. — Какъ страшна не смерть — я её привѣтствую, — а неизбѣжная старость!

Померанцевъ мнѣ посвятилъ свой романсъ. Танеевъ мнѣ привезъ свои дуэты. Буду опять заниматься музыкой.

Погода мѣняется; эту недѣлю была страшная жара, а сегодня тепло, но дождь маленькiй и вѣтеръ къ вечеру.

Какая была теплая, свѣтлая и радостная недѣля, еслибъ не горе отъ Тани!

14 Іюня 1897 г. (31)

Съ утра и весь день проявляла фотографіи,
копировала и ра= =ботала на верху,
что меня просили. Вотъ и мой портретъ,
вырѣзывала изъ не= удачной группы съ
гранѣй. Но говорятъ, что я моложавѣе этого
портрета, это отъ того, что у меня яркія
краски въ лицѣ. — Ходили къ вечеру купаться, сѣверный вѣтеръ и ясное небо. Вечеромъ
устала, Л. Н. меня позвалъ прогуляться,
чему я была очень рада. Миша неожи-
данно откровенно и горячо началъ мнѣ

мнѣ 53 года.

разсказывать о томъ, какъ ему стало трудно отъ
полового возбужденія, какъ онъ чувствуетъ себя даже
больнымъ, желалъ бы остаться чистымъ и боится, что
не устоитъ. Бѣдные мои мальчики! Я имъ плохой
отецъ, и что я могу совѣтовать въ такихъ дѣлахъ?
Я ничего не знаю изъ этой области мужской жизни.
Таня была въ Тулѣ. Левъ Никол. веселъ, разсказы-
валъ, какъ онъ въ Тулѣ заѣхалъ на велосипедѣ
въ ~~…~~ велосипедный кругъ и всѣ разговоры о гонкахъ
и (всемъ, что касается велосипедной ѣзды. Его
и это еще интересуетъ! — Чувствую себя вялой,
писала письмо Лёвѣ, отвѣчала на разныя дѣло-
выя, выдавала жалованье, записывала счеты, и
немного переписала для Л. Н.а его статьи
„Объ искусствѣ." Бодрость и плодотворная дѣятельность.
Переписывала для Л. Н. до 3х часовъ ночи.

YASNAYA POLYANA, 1896

Self-Portraits

"Today we had a discussion about photography, as I have bought a camera and intend to do landscapes and family portraits." 2 July 1887

YASNAYA POLYANA, 1906

THE SELF-PORTRAIT AT LEFT is a metaphor for how Sonya often understood her plight: She is alone, contained, isolated in her own private world. Her husband looms over her.

It is fitting to begin the story of Sonya and her photography with her self-portraits. Though she was dedicated to photographing her husband, self-portraiture was her most basic, enduring theme. She began photographing in earnest 48 years after the first Daguerrotypes were unveiled in Paris in 1839, when photography was physically difficult and and aesthetically insecure. But she found a way to express herself directly in her self-portraits, looking inward, not only outward.

She was without her usual concern for the opinions of the scores of strong people in her life: She photographed herself unsentimentally, romantically, playfully, in clothes her husband didn't approve of, and in poses and compositions that were experimental and uninhibited for her day.

She had no remote control device on her camera, but she trusted and felt at ease with family and friends who were nearby while she was photographing and any who came along at her request to trigger the shutter. Volunteers were not hard to come by. She didn't keep a record of who pressed the button for any given picture—it just wasn't important.

The personal world Sonya creates in her self-portraits is untroubled and calm; her solitary photographic moments aren't lonely or dissatisfied. She connects forthrightly with prospective viewers. She is open, her sense of self is strong, and so is her capacity for intimacy.

Sonya's diary, frequently showing another, unhappier mood, rounds out the picture her photographs present. She first began writing a diary when she was 11 years old. Tolstoy kept a diary, too. Sonya burned hers shortly before their marriage; Tolstoy showed his wife-to-be his diaries a week before their wedding day with the intention that they begin their life together without secrets. Eighteen-year-old Sonya never got over her horror at her groom's sexual exploits, but her love weathered the traumatic episode.

She began writing a new diary shortly after her wedding, and she kept it up, with lapses, until her last entry on November 9, 1910, two days after Tolstoy died. Her diary frequently shows an unhappy mood, which is different from that in her photographs, For example:

DIARY ENTRY **15 July 1897**

...I long passionately for music, and to play myself. But there's never any time, and besides Lev Nikolaevich is always working or sleeping, and every sound disturbs him. I try to convince myself that true happiness comes from fulfilling one's duty, and I force myself to copy out all his writings and do all my other duties, but sometimes I weaken, and yearn for some personal happiness, a private life and work of my own, rather than constantly toiling away for others as I have done for the whole of my life.... And then the feeling goes and I feel wretched.

Other Photographers | # Self-portraiture

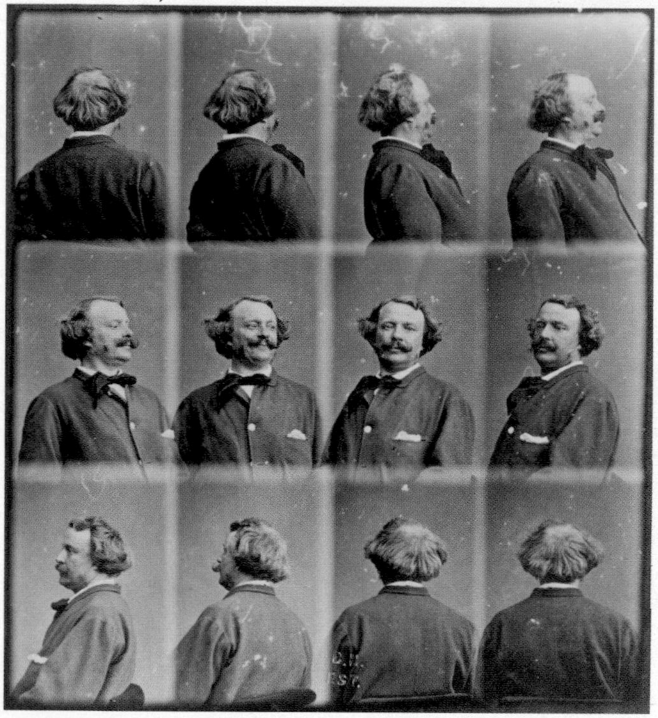

NADAR (FELIX TOURNACHON), CIRCA 1865

SELF-PORTRAITURE in photography was an uncommon practice when Sonya took it up. The reason was at least partly technical: Remote control was awkward, if not impossible, and having somebody nearby to trigger the shutter when the mood struck or the moment was just so was inconvenient and inhibiting for most photographers.

One of the very few professionals to experiment with self-portraits in those early days was the Frenchman Felix Tournachon, known as Nadar, a bold, imaginative man who took the first aerial photographs from a hot-air balloon in 1858 and two years later, using electric lights, made pictures of Parisian sewers. But it was as a portrait photographer that he was renowned. His subjects were artists, composers, and writers, including Russia's Ivan Turgenev, who lived in Paris in the 1850s. Tolstoy, who had an uneasy friendship with Turgenev, briefly visited him during that period and socialized with his aristocratic ex-pat friends.

In 1855, apparently in an experimental mood, Nadar turned his camera on himself. He obviously wanted to record his physical self sympathetically, but also with clinical directness and accuracy: He placed himself against a blank background and blended a studied, casual posture with formal framing. Still photographing himself against a blank background ten years later, he produced a 12-part grid showing himself slowly revolving. Again the goal was straightforward—to study, with nearly ethnographic precision, the nuances of his face and profile, including even the back of his head.

SONYA TOLSTOY: SELF-PORTRAIT WITH ANNA MASLOVA, SELISHCHE ESTATE, JULY 13, 1898

ANDREI KARELIN, CIRCA 1870/6

Sonya was after a more romantic result than Nadar's. She frequently photographed herself simply to mark an event or satisfy the request of a visitor but found ways to turn such events into something more, playing the star in her own thoughtfully shaped settings, an actress in a story that was truthful but idealized. She wasn't the reclusive type. She responded to praise, and when her own desires dovetailed with those in her circle asking for pictures she was pleased. Photography as a social experience wasn't enough however; she also photographed herself in solitary situations, for personal reasons.

Russian photographer Andrei Osipovich Karelin, seven years older than Sonya, was closer to home and to her sensibility than Nadar was. Karelin began devising stage-managed scenes for his camera shortly before Sonya started photographing seriously. His pictures, influenced by the works of Vermeer, Steen, and other Dutch genre painters, were exquisitely contrived; his refined lighting, his stilted poses (in which his subjects resemble props at times), and his controlled composition delivered a gorgeous, sometimes poetic, artificiality. During the 1870s and 1880s his widely praised work won awards in Paris, Philadelphia, Edinburgh, and Moscow.

Self-portraiture was not a primary interest of Karelin's, but he did make a few pictures of himself. The self-portraits he made were fanciful—Sonya had that in common with him. And like Karelin, Sonya depicted herself theatrically. But her poses were less slick and self-conscious than Karelin's. Without his artificial lighting and various other professional tools the result was not nearly as technically sophisticated.

But the lack of absolute technical control contributes to a feeling of realism in Sonya's work. Fantasy for her is a device for getting to the heart of things. Sonya, like many painters, and later photographers, used self-portraiture to examine her own likeness, explore her feelings, and ultimately investigate her personal identity. But she did these things lightly. She never considered herself a fine artist and didn't really expect to make portraits that would deeply penetrate the soul—hers or anybody else's. Her approach was direct and emotional, and though she was smart, her pictures weren't strongly intellectual. At the core she remained a documentarian, a diarist, mixing factuality with her inner world of imagination to record and express her own life—she felt impelled to do this rather than to reach for an earlier, painterly myth.

Sonya didn't participate in any organizations, but she stayed abreast of developments in the newly blossoming field of photography. In her own informal way she was part of a worldwide amateur photography movement. Photography, technically challenging, required devotion and quite a bit of skill from these amateur, non-commercial practitioners who traveled widely, had passionate views on the social, technical, and artistic possibilities of photography, and had their own periodicals and societies through which they shared, exhibited, and exchanged work.

In the best of Sonya's photographs she seems close to us; often she looks directly into the camera, as if openly surrendering herself to a relationship with the viewer. More than half a century passed before photographers attempted self-portraiture anything like Sonya's.

ANDREI KARELIN, CIRCA 1890/4

THIRTY YEARS BEFORE she made the photograph opposite, Sonya recorded a day's torment over clashing values and wishes; the picture is evidence of one of her enduring desires—to dress up in fine clothes and be admired for her beauty.

DIARY ENTRY **13 February 1873**

Lyovochka has gone to Moscow and all day long I have been sitting alone here wretchedly staring into space, a prey to sickening anxieties which leave me no peace. I always take up my diary when I am in this sort of mental turmoil, for I can pour out all my emotions and then feel calmer. But my present mood is sinful, stupid, spiteful and insincere. Where would I be without the support of this good honest man, whom I love with all my heart, and whose thoughts are always so fine and pure? Yet in moments of anxiety I sometimes search my heart and ask myself what I really want. And to my horror, the answer is that I want gaiety, smart clothes and chatter. I want people to admire me and say how pretty I am, and I want Lyova to see and hear them too; I long for him to occasionally emerge from his rapt inner existence which demands so much of him; I wish he could briefly lead a normal life with me, like a normal person. But then my heart cries out against the Devil's temptations of Eve, and I think even worse of myself than before.... I want to turn my character inside out and demolish everything that is mean and false in me. I am having my hair curled today, and have been happily imagining how nice it will look, even though nobody will see me and it is quite unnecessary. I adore ribbons, I would like a new leather belt—and now I have written this I feel like crying....The children are waiting upstairs for their music lesson and here I am in the study writing all this stupid nonsense...

When Sonya wrote this she was 28, the mother of six children, still pretty with dark eyes and a glowing complexion. She was emotional about daily domestic events, a dreamer, and prone to outbursts of temper.

She had grown up pampered and idealistic, given an education in Russian literature, history, French, music, and painting. She and her sisters had attended balls and lively entertainments as soon as they were old enough. On her wedding day in 1862, she was a slender, radiant girl. Her concept of marriage was childishly romantic. She had no idea of what she was getting into, but she was forced to grow up quickly. Lev Tolstoy was uniquely complicated, passionate, and demanding.

She poured her overflowing emotions into her babies as they arrived one after another. But according to her sister Tanya's memoirs:

Sonya never gave herself up completely to the gaiety or happiness with which her youth and early years of marriage were blessed. She somehow did not trust her happiness, did not know how to grasp it and exploit it to the full. It always seemed to her that at any moment something would interfere with it, or that something else must be added to make her happiness perfect. This trait of her character remained with her as long as she lived. Father knew this trait in her character and used to say: Poor little Sonya will never be entirely happy.

Gradually Sonya grew to love rural Yasnaya Polyana, the Tolstoy ancestral home where her husband brought her immediately after their wedding. But she never stopped loving to dress elegantly. She photographed herself in the fashionable outfit opposite in August 1903, but only wore it that one time because Tolstoy detested it.

YASNAYA POLYANA, AUGUST 1903

MOSCOW, WINTER, 1898

DIARY ENTRY **12 February 1898**

I wrote to Masha yesterday. It's her 27th birthday today. And to think she's my fifth! I can never feel old—I am still young in every respect: in my eagerness for work, my impressionability, my capacity for love and grief, my passion for music, my delight in skating and parties. My step is light, my body is fit—only my face has aged...

Diary entries and photographs made during the 1890s bear witness to Sonya's energy, strong opinions, loving nature, inner turmoil, humanity, and vanity—even after giving birth to 13 children.

Sonya's indomitable personality was out of step with her husband's expectations. Tolstoy accepted the popular view that women were inferior to men, declaring even to his own sons that the most intelligent woman was less intelligent than the most limited man. Actually both husband and wife had blind spots in their social outlook. Socially conservative Sonya accepted many of the prevailing, non-egalitarian views of the day—her diary suggests that she was an elitist, somewhat bigoted and anti-Semitic, but that ultimately she didn't give these matters much thought.

Year by year Tolstoy's personally crafted social mission was taking him further away from Sonya. In 1898, the year of this photograph and the above diary entry, two of Tolstoy's projects were concluded, his work on behalf of the Dukhobors, a religious sect persecuted because they refused military service, and his book titled What Is Art? in which he declares art must serve a social purpose.

Sonya vehemently disagreed with Tolstoy's views on art. For her, the purpose of art was to respond to spiritual concerns, not to express political or social needs.

She was of two minds about the Dukhobors. She didn't object to giving them limited funds, but thought Tolstoy wasn't worried enough about the financial needs of his own children. Tolstoy had raised money from his writing to send 2,000 Dukhobors to Canada to start a new life. Son Sergei accompanied them on the journey. Possibly influenced by him, Sonya wrote in her diary:

DIARY ENTRY **26 December 1898**

A letter from Seryozha with a wonderful description of the Dukhobors' departure...I worry about him, but his is a good cause, noble, interesting and just....According to Seryozha, there was something truly terrible and triumphant about their departure. They sang hymns, the steamer cast off—and who knows what awaits this population...setting off on a twenty-five day journey for places unknown, without knowing the language and without money...What astonishing fortitude.

Three months earlier, Sonya made a diary entry summing up her view of her relationship with her husband.

DIARY ENTRY **23 September 1898**

My wedding anniversary. Today I have been married to Lev Nikolaevich for 36 years—and we are apart. It saddens me that we are not closer. I have made so many attempts to achieve some spiritual intimacy with him! There is a strong bond between us—I only wish it was based on something more congenial. But I am not complaining; it is good that he's so concerned about me, guards me so jealously and is so afraid of losing me. With no cause.

YASNAYA POLYANA, JULY 10, 1900

YASNAYA POLYANA, JULY 10, 1900 (VARIANT)

YASNAYA POLYANA, JULY 10, 1900 (VARIANT)

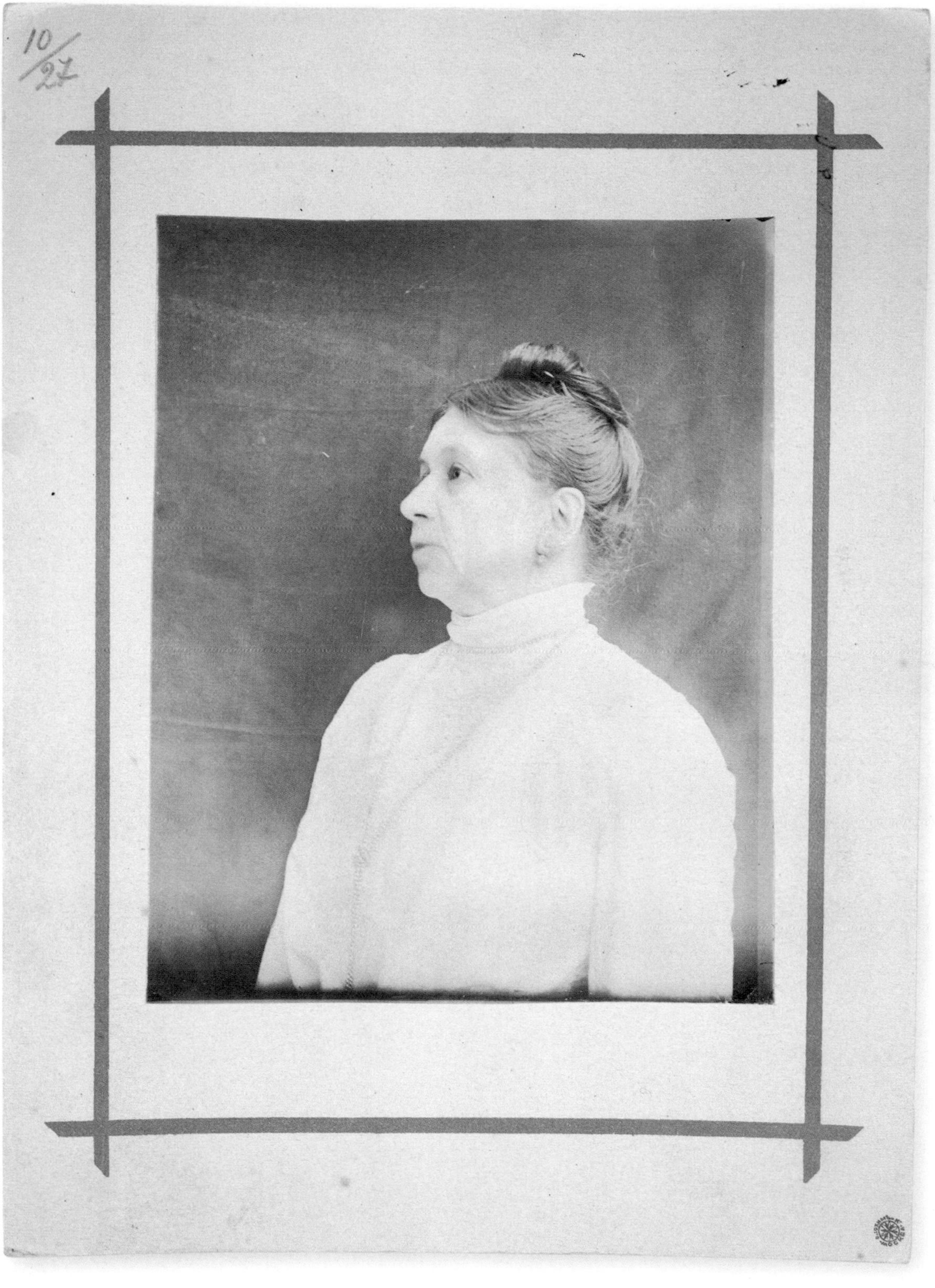

YASNAYA POLYANA, AUGUST 1903

ONE REASON SONYA MADE self-portraits was to fill requests from artists who wished to depict her in plaster, bronze, or paint. The pictures she gave them for reference in response to their requests reflect her own ideas and were sometimes better than the products of the artists she created them for. She worked collaboratively with the artists who came to the estate and though she didn't always like their work, she understood them. Artists, for their part, were eager to work at the Tolstoys' and some turned up over and over again.

The four photographs on the previous pages are cleanly composed and far from mere clinical recordings of features and postures. The first three in this sequence show Sonya's face emerging on the photographic paper submerged in chemical developer; she is gradually allowing herself to be seen. The partial revelations emphasize her eyes, facial features, and profile. The composition shifts in the third frame and the printing process is completed. There is a purity, almost a girlishness about Sonya in the white setting with her hair down. She made the three white prints on July 10, 1900, for the artist Naum Lvovich Aronson.

A few years later Sonya chose the same framing and posture for another self-portrait; this time she darkened the background and finished her coiffure. She thought enough of all four photographs to frame them. The act of framing marks her respect for the creative process and her appreciation for the distinctive qualities of works-in-progress, as perfect in their way as the final, finished work. Sonya wrote about Aronson in her diary just once:

DIARY ENTRY **14 June 1901**

We…have staying here a sculptor named Aronson, a poor Jew who has spent the last eight years in Paris turning himself into an accomplished sculptor. He is doing busts of Lev Nikolaevich and me, and a bas-relief of Tanya—they're not too bad either. He hasn't made me look as hideous as all the artists have done. I don't know why it is that although people generally find me quite pretty, all the portraits, photographs and busts of me are really very ugly. They say one can never catch the expression in a face, the sparkle in the eyes, the color of the skin and the irregularity of the features.

NAUM LVOVICH ARONSON: SOPHIA TOLSTOY, YASNAYA POLYANA

THE ARTIST LEONID OSIPOVICH PASTERNAK makes his first appearance in Sonya's diary in October 1898. The occasion was Lev Tolstoy's desire to have drawings made of scenes from his novel *Resurrection* for publication in the French journal *Illustration*. Sonya didn't think much of *Resurrection* but she saw in Pasternak a man who was "lively, clever, educated."

Tolstoy wrote *Resurrection* at the end of the 1890s to raise money to move the persecuted Dukhobors to Canada. The novel is based upon an actual legal case described to Tolstoy by St. Petersburg lawyer, A.F. Koni. Tolstoy was so impressed by the case he asked Koni to write it out for him: A prostitute convicted of murder was exiled to Siberia; during the trial that led to her conviction one of the jurors recognized her as a woman he had seduced when they were young; he was filled with remorse for his responsibility in her downfall.

Ten years after the incident occurred Tolstoy fictionalized the story to condemn Russia's justice and penal systems and to expound his radical ideas about sex and religion. (He had arrived at an ascetic philosophy that called for giving away his possessions and repudiating sex.) Sonya abhorred these views; furthermore, she found *Resurrection*'s characters unconvincing. On September 12, she wrote in her diary:

DIARY ENTRY **12 September 1898**

This morning L.N. read us Resurrection, the story he is currently working on. I had heard it before—he said he had reworked it, but it's still exactly the same. He read it to us three years ago....And then as now I was struck by the beauty of the incidental details and episodes, and the hypocrisy of the novel itself—Nekhlyudov's relationship with the prostitute in jail and the author's own attitude to her. It's just sentimentality, toying with strained, unnatural feelings which don't really exist.

In spite of these feelings Sonya devoted herself to helping Tolstoy prepare the manuscript for publication.

Pasternak's devotion to Lev Tolstoy extended to his family and he conscientiously applied himself to depicting Sonya and the children. Sonya took these two pictures for him in 1900 and made a note in her register of negatives: "All for a pose at the insistence of artist Pasternak." It is not known how much Pasternak stage directed these, but Sonya is engrossed and careful in her performance and clearly enjoyed the theatrical opportunity.

YASNAYA POLYANA, 1900

YASNAYA POLYANA, 1900 (VARIANT)

YASNAYA POLYANA, JUNE 1901

SONYA MADE THIS PHOTOGRAPH OF HERSELF writing at an outdoor table for Pasternak about a year after she made him the two pictures of herself posing with the luxuriant bouquet. She didn't caption her pictures very deeply, so we don't know what she's writing or thinking. She considered such particulars unimportant to the photograph, especially when staging a scene rather than documenting one. The visual success of the pose was what mattered here.

Her thoughts and opinions were matters for her written diary where she also meticulously recorded the episodes in her married life from the beginning. When she began photographing more than two decades later, it was to deal with the same subjects she had been writing about, but in a different way. The photographs added to the factual content of her written diary and expressed different moods.

At first she wrote spontaneously, though somewhat self-consciously, about her feelings for Lev Nikolaevich, or Lyovochka—she used both these names—and she poured out her feelings about their relationship.

Both husband and wife used their diaries to communicate, saying things they didn't dare say aloud to one another:

DIARY ENTRY (LEV) **8 January 1863**

In the morning—her clothes. She challenged me to object to them, and I did object, and said so—tears and vulgar explanations....We patched things up somehow. I'm always dissatisfied with myself on these occasions, especially with the kisses—they are false patches....I feel that she is depressed, but I'm more depressed still, and I can't say anything to her—there's nothing to say. I'm just cold, and I clutch at any work with ardor. She will stop loving me. I'm almost certain of that. The one thing that can save me is if she doesn't fall in love with someone else, and that won't be my doing. She says I'm kind. I don't like to hear it; it's just for that reason that she will stop loving me.

DIARY ENTRY (SONYA) **9 January 1863**

Never in my life have I felt so wretched with remorse. Never did I imagine that I could be so much to blame. I have been choked with tears all day. I feel so depressed. I am afraid to talk to him or look at him....I am sure he must suddenly have realized just how vile and pathetic I am.

DIARY ENTRY (LEV) **15 January 1863**

Got up late; we're on friendly terms. The last squabble has left some small (imperceptible) traces—or perhaps time has. Every such squabble, however trivial, is a scar on love. A momentary feeling of passion, vexation, self-love or pride will pass, but a scar, however small, will remain forever on the best thing that exists in the world—love. I shall know this and guard our happiness, and you know it too...

DIARY ENTRY (LEV) **5 August 1863**

...I've looked through her diary—suppressed anger with me glows beneath words of tenderness. It's often the same in real life. If this is so, and it's all a mistake on her part—it's terrible...

Almost three decades after this exchange Sonya decided to copy her husband's diary for posterity. She noted on November 20, 1890,
I have been copying Lyovochka's diaries, which cover

his whole life.... She described how the copying job affected her.

DIARY ENTRY (SONYA) **8 December 1890**

I am still copying out Lyovochka's diary. Why did I never read and copy it before? It has simply been lying in my chest of drawers all this time. I don't think I ever recovered from the shock of reading Lyovochka's diaries when I was engaged to him—I can still remember the agonizing pangs of jealousy, the horror of that first appalling experience of male depravity...

Sonya seems to have photographed mostly when she was happy and written mostly when she was depressed, but not always. Her only entry for the year 1868 reads:

DIARY ENTRY **31 July 1868**

It makes me laugh to read my diary. What a lot of contradictions—as though I were the unhappiest of women! But who could be happier? When I'm alone in the room I sometimes laugh for joy and cross myself, and pray to God for many, many more years of happiness. I always write in my diary when we quarrel....and we wouldn't quarrel if we didn't love one another....I have been married for six years now....but I still love him with the same passionate, poetic, fevered, jealous love...

Twenty years later both their diaries are filled with bitter accusations and anguish. At the end Tolstoy hid his diaries from Sonya, and she, in a state of paranoia, searched obsessively for them.

WITH LEV TOLSTOY, YASNAYA POLYANA, 1895

SONYA MADE THIS ENTRY in her diary on February 23, 1895, after the unthinkable had happened.:
My darling little Vanechka died this evening at 11 o'clock. My God, and I am still alive!

Vanechka, the Tolstoys' 13th and last child, died from scarlet fever a month before he turned seven. Even 11-year-old Sasha, the next-to-youngest with seemingly justifiable reasons to be jealous, had adored this little brother.

Sonya, painfully estranged from her husband because of his increasingly extreme views about marriage and property, poured love into Vanechka in a manner some said was excessive, spending hours on end with him, neglecting Sasha and the others. And Vanechka at age six could read her moods and knew how to love her in return. Sonya constantly feared for him and had dire premonitions, one of them four years before he died when he was three, down with a childhood infection:

DIARY ENTRY **9 January 1891**
This evening...I carried Vanechka about in my arms, as he had lost his voice. What a gentle, affectionate, sensitive, clever little boy he is! I love him more than anything in the world and am terrified that he will not live long.

Tolstoy loved Vanechka as tenderly as the others did and believed this child would be the one to grow up to carry on his work. Overcome with grief when Vanechka died, he stood sobbing in the churchyard as the coffin was lowered into the grave. After the funeral, Tolstoy drew close to Sonya for a brief time and tried to comfort her, but she was inconsolable. Sonya's religious feelings ran deep but, unlike her husband's, they didn't provide solace for this loss. Three days after Vanechka's death Tolstoy wrote in his diary:
We've buried Vanechka. A terrible—no, not a terrible, but a great spiritual event. I thank Thee Father. I thank Thee.

In spring Sonya wrote her sister Tanya:
There is nothing for me: not nature or sun or flowers....not riches or even children. All is dead and everything is a ghastly bore.

A few months later, in August, she wrote Tanya again:
I have taken up photography in order to run away from myself, but my progress is slow. I would like to photograph Vanechka's and my favorite places in Yasnaya Polyana. I'll do my best...

That fall, on October 25th, Tolstoy recorded his concern in his diary:
I wish she wasn't so depressed, sad, lonely. For her there's only me to hold onto.... you are not alone, I'm with you just as you are, I love and love you to the utmost, no one can love more.

At the back of the house, on the porch, Sonya arranged Vanechka's favorite toys under his portrait to resemble an icon corner; she walked into her still-life and photographed herself grieving.

WITH PORTRAIT OF VANECHKA, YASNAYA POLYANA, 1897

WHEN VANECHKA DIED, Sonya stopped writing in her diary altogether for two years. She resumed writing in June 1897. In one of her first entries, on June 15, 1897, she wrote:
I didn't sleep a wink all night. Towards morning I dozed off, but was shaken awake by my own sobbing. I was dreaming of Vanechka; Nurse and I were going through all his toys, and I was weeping...

During the years Sonya wasn't writing she gradually began photographing more seriously than before. Photography (and also music) absorbed her and provided a refuge and outlet, at least to some degree. But she was burdened with self-doubt and conflict about photography: She didn't have a lot of confidence in her talent and she felt guilty spending time on personal pursuits. Nevertheless, when she took up her diary again she had woven photography seamlessly, though inconsistently, into her everyday life:

DIARY ENTRY **19 June 1897**
The moment I got up this morning I made prints of my photographs of Sasha and Vetochka...

DIARY ENTRY **13 July 1897**
...Turkin and I took photographs of everyone yesterday and today, and most of mine came out very well indeed. I took a lot of Sergei Ivanovich and Lev Nikolaevich didn't mind so much this time...

DIARY ENTRY **15 July 1897**
I got up late, developed some prints, then went swimming with Sasha and the governesses. Afterwards I did some more developing...and gave Sasha her lesson, which went very well today...

DIARY ENTRY **16 July 1897**
I spent the evening pasting photographs into the album. I shall give them all away tomorrow, and shan't waste any more of my time on my photography. I did about 80.

Sonya had apparently tapped into a phenomenon unique to photography: It can simultaneously engage and distance the photographer from a subject. This was just what Sonya needed. The camera physically provided her a safe emotional separation from her everyday life, but in order to compose and light effectively, her complete attention was called for. Sonya's nature demanded action; photography provided a place to put her emotional and physical energy.

DIARY ENTRY **17 July 1897**
I did more copying [of Tolstoy's manuscripts] and developed more photographs. I gave them all away today, and shall soon give up this hobby.

DIARY ENTRY **20 July 1897**
I stayed up late working on some photographs which had come out unsuccessfully...I played the piano for an hour both yesterday and today, but it's not enough!

DIARY ENTRY **21 August 1897**
I took photographs all yesterday and today—flowers, the apple harvest, the apple trees, a hut and so on.

DIARY ENTRY **23 August 1897**
I waste my time on unsuccessful photographs and do no copying which makes me feel very guilty...

VORONKA RIVER, NEAR YASNAYA POLYANA, 1897

POLISH PIANIST WANDA LANDOWSKA WITH TOLSTOY, HALL IN YASNAYA POLYANA, 1907

Music & Poetry

"I long desperately for music; I'd like to play myself, but I never have the time. I did play two of Mendelssohn's 'Songs Without Words' today, however. Oh, those songs! One of them in particular moves me to my very soul." **7 June 1897**

"I played the piano for four hours today; music lifts me off the ground and makes all my worries and difficulties easier to bear." **30 July 1897**

SERGEI IVANOVICH TANEYEV, a short, stout bachelor with a bushy red beard, was known for his legendary piano performances. His virtuoso interpretations of Tchaikovsky, with whom he had studied, seemed literally to cast a spell over his admiring audiences. Sonya and he were involved in a platonic love affair, innocent and fervent, that lasted the better part of a decade.

Sonya first made Taneyev's acquaintance in Moscow in the mid 1880s. She had taken her children to the city for their education and engaged Taneyev to teach her musically gifted son Seryozha. Sonya knew Taneyev as a composer and director of the Moscow Conservatory, but didn't see him on stage until she attended a concert in Kiev in April 1895, two months or so after the death of Vanechka. She was enthralled by the performance. Under the musical enchantment of that evening, and then during the many hours she subsequently spent with Taneyev, she found a haven (in some ways easier than photography) from the anguish of losing Vanechka and from her marriage, which had become increasingly filled with bitter arguments over Tolstoy's views about property and lifestyle.

After the memorable concert Sonya looked for every opportunity to be in Taneyev's presence. She visited him in Moscow and St. Petersburg and invited him for visits and family outings in Yasnaya Polyana. She attended as many of his performances and rehearsals as possible and arranged to take piano lessons from him. She was vivacious in his company, dressed elegantly, photographed him, and filled her diary with thoughts of him.

Her daughters disapproved: They stopped short of accusing their mother of immorality but thought her behavior unseemly and inappropriate. As time went by Tolstoy became increasingly agitated by his wife's ardent attachment. He made his feelings clear repeatedly. He wrote the following letter from a friend's estate, where he and daughter Tanya had gone for a visit:

Nikolskoye-Obolyanovo, February 1, 1897
My dear Sonya,

Tanya has written to you about our journey here and how we are, about our outer state, but I want to write to you about what interests you—my inner, spiritual state.

I was sad when I was leaving, and you felt it, and for that reason came to the station, but you didn't dispel my miserable feeling but rather made it worse. You told me to be calm and then said that you wouldn't go to the rehearsal. I couldn't understand for a long time what rehearsal. I'd never even thought about it. And all this hurts me. It was unpleasant—more than unpleasant—for me to learn that in spite of the fact that you spent so much time considering when to go to Petersburg and making preparations, the result is that you are going just at the time when there was no need to go....This game is terribly painful to me. You may say that you couldn't have organized the visit differently. But if you think about it and analyze yourself, you will see that it isn't true: firstly, there is no particular need for the journey, and secondly, you could have gone before or after—during Lent.

But you can't help doing this. It's terribly painful and humiliatingly shameful that a complete outsider, an unnecessary and quite uninteresting man, rules our life and poisons the last years or year of our life; it's humiliating and painful that one has to ask when and where he is going, and when he is playing at what rehearsals.

This is terrible, terrible, shameful and repulsive. And

COMPOSER AND PIANIST SERGEI TANEYEV, YASNAYA POLYANA, 1907

SERGEI TANEYEV, 1898 (BOTH)

it's happening just at the end of our life—a life spent well and purely—just at the time when we have been drawing closer and closer together in spite of everything that could divide us. This rapprochement began long ago, even before Vanechka's death, and became closer and closer, especially recently, and suddenly, instead of a natural, good and joyful conclusion to 35 years of life together, there is this repulsive vileness which has left its terrible imprint on everything. I know you are miserable and you are suffering too because you love me and want to be good, but so far you can't, and I'm terribly sorry for you because I love you with the best kind of love—not of the body or the mind, but of the soul.

Goodbye, and forgive me dearest.

I kiss you.

L. T.

But Sonya's feelings for Taneyev continued to deepen and according to her diary, so did Tolstoy's loathing for the man.

DIARY ENTRY **5 June 1897**

Sergei Ivanovich left today, and Lev Nikolaevich immediately became calm and cheerful again....It is only because Lev Nikolaevich is suffering that he makes these jealous demands that I have nothing more to do with Sergei Ivanovich. But to break off relations with him would make me suffer too. I feel so little guilt and so much calm joy in my pure peaceful friendship with this man, that I could no more tear him out of my heart than I could stop seeing, breathing or thinking.

DIARY ENTRY **4 July 1897**

...After dinner there were...painful discussions, accusations of lying and demands that I either extinguish my special feelings for Sergei Ivanovich or break off all relations with him. Both suggestions are utterly preposterous. One cannot simply extinguish the feeling one has for a person. As for actions, which are under one's control, I have done nothing I could be reproached with....

Meanwhile life went on as usual in the Tolstoy household. Sonya kept up her diverse and complicated family responsibilities and social obligations. Her relationship with Taneyev wasn't always smooth, and she agonized over that along with everything else.

DIARY ENTRY **24 November 1897**

...I took Lyova's article—a translation from the Swedish—to the Russian Gazette.

I got home, changed, then went off to a name-day celebration for Dunaev, Davydov and Ermolov. I love this worldly brilliance, lovely clothes, masses of flowers, refined company, cultured conversation and good manners. As always, as at every age in my life, there was general astonishment at my unusually youthful appearance....I got back and played the piano for about an hour and a half. This evening Raevskii came with my brother Petya and his daughter. Tonight I played the piano again, from midnight until 2 a.m. I do so want to make progress, but I can never find the time. Seryozha played very nicely. 10° of frost, there's a moon.

Sergei Ivanovich hasn't once come to see me. He must have heard reports about L. N.'s jealously, and his cordiality toward me has changed to extreme coldness. How sad, and how sorry I am! There is no other possible explanation for his aloofness—why else would he not come to visit? Could L. N. have written to him?

It is unlikely that Tolstoy wrote to Taneyev. Though Tolstoy thought Taneyev "an unnecessary and quite uninteresting man," Taneyev admired

Tolstoy very much and said so to Sonya in a letter to her on August 27, 1898, on the occasion of Tolstoy's 70th birthday:

I am thankful to him for a great deal of what I've read from his works and brought away from my association with him. There is no need to be a 'follower' of Lev Nikolaevich in order to experience the impact of his clear, simple and enduring ideas, which once sunk deep into the mind, very persistently stay there, sometimes considerably disturbing a man by raising demands that exceed his strength.

Sonya's relationship with Taneyev was both less and more than a romance. Her frustrated lifelong desire for a creative outlet was expressed, powerfully for a time, through her feelings for the musician. In a diary entry during this period she wrote, "*Taneyev played two of Mendelsohn's 'Songs Without Words' and my heart turned over within me...*" Between 1895 and 1900 she wrote a barely fictionalized account of their affair and titled the novella *Song Without Words* after Felix Mendelssohn's piece.

The story tells of a heroine, Alexandra Alexeyevna, who lives with her husband, Pyotr Afanasevych, an insurance company clerk in Moscow. Alexandra is busy with the family and with her son Alyosha. Pyotr gives his heart and time to his favorite horticultural projects.

When Alexandra receives news that her mother is gravely ill, she travels to the Crimea to be with her. Before long her mother dies, a heavy blow to the heroine.

Unable to resume daily life in the city, Alexandra leaves for her summer dacha. Her next-door neighbor happens to be Ivan Ilych, a highly talented musician. The first composition Alexandra hears him play is "Song Without Words." The music, full of feeling, brings her back to life and fills her existence with meaning.

Now the heroine begins to give practically all her time to Ivan. Their shared worship of high art, lofty emotions, and feelings of spiritual affinity gradually lead Alexandra to a deep infatuation with Ivan's personality and writings.

But Alexandra is torn with remorse. She goes to a priest to make confession—an insincere formality it turns out—then she visits a convent.

[A parallel by-plot features an acquaintance of Alexandra's family who gives up military service and to whom many pages are devoted.]

Back in Moscow, the heroine remains fascinated by Ivan and music. Her husband, realizing what is going on, nobly seeks to overcome his feelings and find a solution to the situation.

But Ivan leaves for the Crimea and gradually drifts away from Alexandra, completely dedicating himself to his art. With thoughts of suicide, the heroine enters a clinic for nervous diseases, where she lingeringly fades away.

Exactly how Taneyev felt about Sonya all this time isn't clear. In the fall of 1904 he began to distance himself from her. At a November concert in Moscow, during the intermission, she accused him of not being attentive enough. They argued and she was extremely hurt. She tried to repair the relationship afterward but was unable to. Overwhelmed by melancholy, she gave up the piano, redoubled her efforts in photography, and spent time on painting as well.

Tanayev died on June 6, 1915. By then Sonya's love for him had long disappeared. She didn't even attend his funeral.

Страхъ и горе
Донынѣ чужды были мнѣ;
Я въ безмятежной тишинѣ,
Въ тѣни гарема расцвѣтала
И первыхъ опытовъ любви
Послушнымъ сердцемъ ожидала.
Желанья тайныя мои
Сбылись. Гирей для мирной нѣги
Войну кровавую презрѣлъ,
Пресѣкъ ужасные набѣги
И свой гаремъ опять узрѣлъ.
Предъ хана въ смутномъ ожиданьѣ
Предстали мы. Онъ свѣтлый взоръ
Остановилъ на мнѣ въ молчаньи,
Позвалъ меня... и съ этихъ поръ
Мы въ безпрерывномъ упоеньѣ
Дышали счастьемъ, и ни разъ
Ни клевета, ни подозрѣнье,
Ни злобной ревности мученье,
Ни скука не смущали насъ.
Марія, ты предъ нимъ явилась..
Увы, съ тѣхъ поръ его душа
Преступной думой омрачилась!
Гирей, измѣною дыша,
Моихъ не слушаетъ укоровъ,
Ему докученъ сердца стонъ;
Ни прежнихъ чувствъ, ни разговоровъ
Со мною не находитъ онъ.
Ты преступленью непричастна,
Я знаю, не твоя вина...
И такъ послушай: я прекрасна;
Во всемъ гаремѣ ты одна
Могла-бъ еще мнѣ быть опасна;
Но я для страсти рождена,
Но ты любить, какъ я, не можешь,
Зачѣмъ же хладной красотой
Ты сердце слабое тревожишь?
Оставь Гирея мнѣ, онъ мой;
На мнѣ горятъ его лобзанья;
Онъ клятвы страшныя мнѣ далъ;
Давно всѣ думы, всѣ желанья
Гирей съ моими сочеталъ;
Меня убьетъ его измѣна...
Я плачу! Видишь, я колѣна
Теперь склоняю предъ тобой,
Молю, винить тебя не смѣя,
Отдай мнѣ радость и покой,
Отдай мнѣ прежняго Гирея.
Не возражай мнѣ ничего;
Онъ мой; онъ ослѣпленъ тобою.
Презрѣньемъ, просьбою, тоскою,
Чѣмъ хочешь, отврати его;
Клянись... (хоть я для Алькорана,
Между невольницами хана,
Забыла вѣру прежнихъ дней,
Но вѣра матери моей
Была твоя) клянись мнѣ сю
Зарему возвратить Гирею...

Но слушай: если я должна
Тебѣ... кинжаломъ я владѣю,
Я близъ Кавказа рождена!

Исп. артистка **Императорскихъ** С.-Петербургскихъ театровъ **Н. А. Фриде.**

а) Чтеніе.

Промчались дни; Маріи нѣтъ,
Мгновенно сирота почила:
Она давно—желанный свѣтъ
Какъ новый ангелъ озарила.
Но что же въ гробъ ее свело?
Тоска-ль неволи безнадежной,
Болѣзнь, или другое зло,
Кто знаетъ? Нѣтъ Маріи нѣжной!...
Дворецъ угрюмый опустѣлъ;
Его Гирей опять оставилъ;
Съ толпой татаръ въ чужой предѣлъ
Онъ злой набѣгъ опять направилъ;
Забытый, преданный презрѣнью,
Не зритъ лица его гаремъ;
Тамъ, обреченныя мученью
И не утѣшены никѣмъ,
Старѣютъ жены. Между ними
Давно грузинки нѣтъ; она
Гарема стражами нѣмыми
Въ пучину водъ опущена.
Въ ту ночь, какъ умерла княжна,
Свершилось и ея страданье.
Какая-бъ ни была вина,
Ужасно было наказанье!...
Опустошивъ огнемъ войны
Кавказу близкія страны
И села мирныя Россіи,
Въ Тавриду возвратился ханъ
И въ память горестной Маріи
Воздвигнулъ мраморный фонтанъ!

5. Заключеніе. Allegro moderato.

Исп. **оркестръ О-ва.**

b) Мелодекламація.

Есть надпись: ѣдкими годами
Еще не сгладилась она.
За чуждыми ея чертами
Журчитъ по мраморѣ вода
И каплетъ хладными слезами,
Не умолкая никогда.
Такъ плачетъ мать во дни печали
О сынѣ, падшемъ на войнѣ.
Младыя дѣвы въ той странѣ
Преданье старины узнали
И мрачный памятникъ онѣ
Фонтаномъ слезъ именовали.

Чтеніе исп. артистка **Императорскихъ** Московскихъ театровъ **Е. Д. Берсъ.**

7. **Гр. Толстой, Л. Н.** . . «КТО ПРАВЪ», рукопись.
Прочтетъ **М. А. Стаховичъ.**

8. **Шопенъ** . . . . Баллада g-moll.
Исп. **А. Б. Гольденвейзеръ.**

9. **Бахъ** . . . . Арія.
Исп. солистъ **Его Императорскаго Величества А. В. Вержбиловичъ.**

Правленіе О-ва покорнѣйше проситъ во время исполненія не входить и не выходить изъ залы.

Рояль фабрики **Бехштейнъ,** изъ магазина **Германъ** и **Гроссманъ.**

Дозволено цензурою. Москва, 13 марта 1901 г.
На основаніи ВЫСОЧАЙШЕ утвержденнаго 5 мая 1892 г. мнѣнія Государственнаго Совѣта и утвержденныхъ 20 августа 1892 г. правилъ взиманія сбора съ публичныхъ зрѣлищъ и увеселеній, со всѣхъ билетовъ взимается сборъ, оплачиваемый марками, безъ коихъ билеты не дѣйствительны.
Печатать разрѣшается. Москва, 16 марта 1901 г. Московск. Оберъ-Полиціймейстеръ Генералъ-Майоръ Треповъ.

Типографія **Императорскихъ** Московскихъ Театровъ — Т-во Скоропечатни А. А. Левенсонъ. Москва.

№ 162

1901

Въ Большомъ залѣ

Россійскаго Благороднаго Собранія

въ Субботу, 17-го Марта,

въ пользу пріюта О-ва попеченія о бѣдныхъ и безпріютныхъ дѣтяхъ въ Москвѣ и ея окружностяхъ, состоящаго подъ попечительствомъ графини **С. А. Толстой,**

ИМѢЕТЪ БЫТЬ

КОНЦЕРТЪ

ОБЩЕСТВА ЛЮБИТЕЛЕЙ

Оркестровой, Камерной и Вокальной Музыки въ Москвѣ,

подъ управленіемъ

А. А. ЛИТВИНОВА.

Начало ровно въ 9 час. вечера.

CONCERT PROGRAM, BENEFIT FOR ORPHANS, SUPPORTED BY SONYA AND LEV TOLSTOY, MARCH 17, 1901

9/34
Иней 27 Ноября 1902 г.
9/34
Mère de toutes les merveilles, douce et tendre nature
pourquoi ne vivons nous pas plus au milieu de toi! (Amiel)

HOARFROST IN OAK WOOD CHEPYZH, YASNAYA POLYANA, NOVEMBER 27, 1902

MUSIC, POETRY, PAINTING, and literature of all kinds gave shape to Sonya's imagination from childhood. Sergei Taneyev enjoyed and benefited from her intelligent appreciation of music, but he was far from the only one whose life was enriched by her enthusiasms.

Sonya's passion for music was also shared by her husband as was her love for literature, the other arts, and her curiosity about human nature. Husband and wife engaged in volatile intellectual arguments or thoughtful conversation and they read aloud in the evenings. They occasionally joined together to sponsor good works, as evidenced by the program for a March 17, 1901, benefit concert for orphaned and impoverished children (page 63). The concert was given by a society having Sonya as a patron. The second page of the program lists musical pieces and also readings, including one by Lev Tolstoy.

Another project the family undertook jointly was the translation of a book by the Swiss philosopher, poet, and critic Henri-Frederic Amiel. Amiel, who died in 1881, was widely known throughout Europe and admired by both Tolstoys. Their son Mikhail Lvovich translated Amiel's book titled *Wonderful Thinkers of the Ancient and Modern World* from French into Russian. Lev Tolstoy wrote a foreword for the New and Revised Edition published in Moscow in 1905.

Amiel's poetic thoughts resonated with Sonya and under this wintry self-portrait she inscribed a quote from him:

Mother of All marvels. Sweet and tender nature, why do we no longer live in your midst!

Both Tolstoys spent many hours searching for the meaning of life. Sonya looked to authoritative texts to help her make sense of the experience of daily living and she read, like she did all other things, with passion. In her diary she noted the books that made the strongest impression and considered their worth for herself personally.

DIARY ENTRY **25 October 1886**

I am reading the lives of the philosophers. It is terribly interesting, but difficult to read calmly and sensibly. One always searches for the philosophical teachings that approximate to one's own convictions, and ignores anything incompatible with them. As a result it is difficult to learn anything new. But I try not to be so prejudiced.

A few years later she recorded, as she had done so often, her appreciation of the nature around her. This time she tried to explain the sense of emptiness and loss she felt in the presence of its beauty; She also seemed to be responding to Amiel.

DIARY ENTRY **9 December 1890**

...Today I went for a walk and thought—it was a marvelous day, 14° below zero, frosty and clear, and every tree, bush and blade of grass was covered in thick snow. I passed the threshing-floor and took the path into the plantation. On my left the sun was already low in the sky, and on my right the moon was rising. The white treetops gleamed, the sky was blue, everything was bathed in rosy light, and in the distant clearing the fluffy snow was dazzling white. What purity. And what a fine and beautiful thing this whiteness and purity is, whether in nature, in one's heart, morals and conscience, or in one's material life. I have tried to preserve it in myself—and all for what? Wouldn't the mere memory of love—however sinful—be preferable to the emptiness of immaculate conscience?

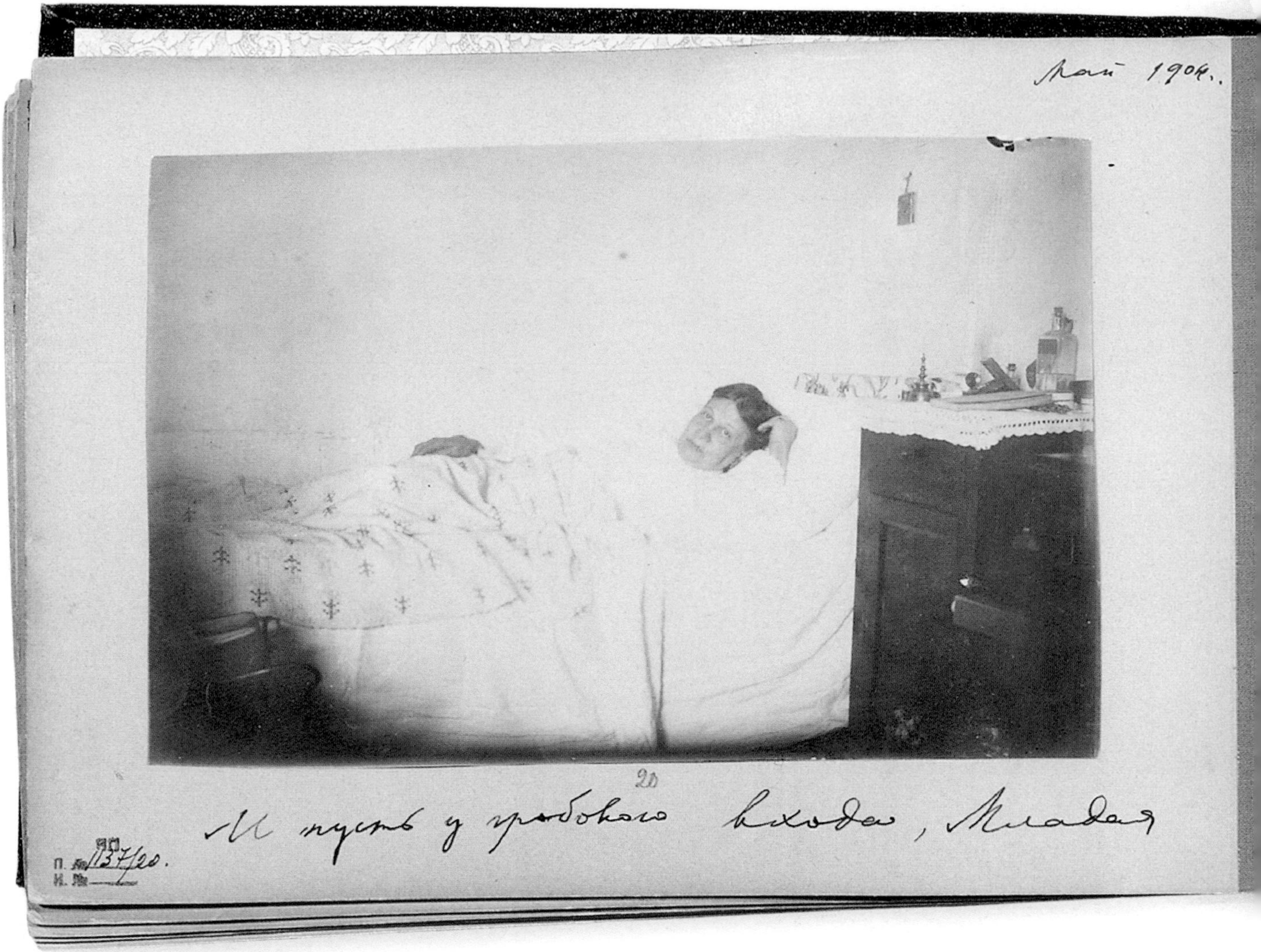

SONYA'S PHOTO ALBUM, MAY 1904 (BOTH)

ON THESE ALBUM PAGES, Sonya juxtaposed two unlike photographs and linked them with a verse by the poet Alexander Sergeyevich Pushkin. She was devoting her photography to expressing the poet's idea of death.

And let at deathly entrance young life be playing,
And indifferent Nature with beauty eternal be blazing.

Alexander Pushkin was Russia's most beloved poet. Sonya admired his work and may have staged her photographs with the idea of joining them with Pushkin's words in a diptych. But that scenario is improbable. It's more likely that she responded to Pushkin's insight about nature's beautiful yet brutal indifference to death by linking the two photographs after she saw them printed. Sonya's impulses were not purely poetic however. She was feeling the pain of Taneyev's sharp coldness at that time and her

despondent mood comes through here.

Pushkin was at the height of his powers about a quarter of a century before Tolstoy wrote his great novels and he was influenced by Pushkin's work. According to his daughter Alexandra he once remarked, "I learn a lot from Pushkin. He is my father; he is the one to learn from." Tolstoy, like Pushkin, was born into a relatively poor aristocratic family. Also like Pushkin he was a romantic who began a historical novel on Peter the Great that was never completed.

Both of these photographs were taken in 1904. One, a self-portrait, shows Sonya "in bed sick." The other is of her grandchildren and their friends, "playing and dancing." 1904 was the year Sonya turned 60, and in addition to her other sorrows she may have had mortality on her mind.

YASNAYA POLYANA, 1902

Lev Tolstoy

"For a genius one has to create a peaceful, cheerful, comfortable home; a genius must be fed, washed and dressed, must have his works copied out innumerable times, must be loved and spared all cause for jealousy, so that he can be calm; then one must feed and educate the innumerable children fathered by this genius, whom he cannot be bothered to care for himself, as he has to commune with all the Epictetuses, Socrateses and Buddhas, and aspire to be like them himself.

And when the members of his family circle have sacrificed their youth, beauty—everything—to serve this genius, they are then blamed for not understanding the geniuses properly—and they never get a word of thanks from the geniuses themselves of course, for sacrificing their pure young lives to him, and atrophying all their spiritual and intellectual capacities, which they are unable to nourish and develop due to lack of peace, leisure and energy." **13 March 1902**

ONE OF SONYA'S CENTRAL PURPOSES in taking pictures—maybe *the* central purpose—was to record Lev Tolstoy for posterity. Early in their marriage she set herself the task of keeping track of his work and delving into his past and making sense of it; she tried hard to do the job justice, but found it disappointingly daunting. On February 27, 1877, she wrote:

As I was reading through some of Lyovochka's old diaries today, I realized I would never be able to write those 'Notes for a Biography,' as I had intended to. His inner life is so complicated and his diaries disturb me so much that I grow confused, and cannot see things clearly. Sadly, I must abandon this dream of mine. I can record our present life, though, and what he says about his intellectual activities, and I shall try not to shirk and to do it conscientiously....

She applied photography wholeheartedly to this record-keeping enterprise: She photographed Tolstoy over and over again, seated, walking, standing, and on horseback, on routine days, special occasions, with family and famous guests, or alone, in various states of health, and engaged in a whole array of activities (though few photographs show him at work because he didn't like to be disturbed).

Tolstoy was an entertaining storyteller and delightful company when he was in good spirits. But in photographs we see an intense, stern man even when lightheartedness would naturally be expected. Whether this was due to the technicalities of a cumbersome photographic process or to Tolstoy's attitude toward the entire enterprise of photography is a matter of speculation.

Experts have scoured the records to decipher Tolstoy's thoughts on this subject as on all other matters. He clearly didn't like to pose. He hated the experience and was against being treated like a celebrity. He was attracted to photography as a young man, but at some point decided it was merely an upper-class toy. Nevertheless, he allowed his picture to be taken quite frequently. He may have tried to hide his resentment toward those who showed up toting cameras, many of them his friends, but the photographs show he didn't usually succeed.

In 1892 Sonya prepared a multi-volume collection of Tolstoy's works. She intended to include a different Tolstoy portrait in each volume, but received a letter from him in which he said, *It is unseemly to print several different portraits of me in the new collected works. Isn't it immodest and awkward to do this in my lifetime?*

Through years when husband and wife were estranged, Tolstoy cooperated with Sonya's photography, apparently signing on to her documentary purpose. In the end he was probably like most of us—he disliked being photographed but liked the pictures afterward. He wanted to look good in them and he treasured photographs of his family and friends.

On evenings when marital relations were harmonious he sat with Sonya, leafing through albums and reminiscing. Here he is returning from a summer walk in the summer of 1905.

RETURNING FROM A SUMMER WALK, YASNAYA POLYANA, 1905

COURTYARD OF KHAMOVNIKI, THE TOLSTOYS' MOSCOW HOUSE, 1898

YASNAYA POLYANA, JULY 15, 1903

DISPATCHING MAIL, LEV TOLSTOY, DAUGHTER SASHA, SONYA, AND GRANDCHILDREN, AUGUST 8, 1903 (BOTH)

Other Photographers

Photographing Tolstoy

TOLSTOY PARTICULARLY LIKED this photograph of himself at work made by Sonya in 1903. In a tribute unusual for him he wrote, "The portrait is beautiful, because there was no posing. The hands are wonderful and the expression is natural." He probably didn't notice his wife photographing him at that moment because he had become accustomed to her "photographic bustle."

Lev Tolstoy spoke 15 languages and read voraciously in many of them; he was an articulate expert in dozens of subjects, a bold activist for social change on behalf of the peasantry, and the author of several of the greatest novels ever written. He was also a bundle of contradictions—first a hunter, then a vegetarian; a womanizer who later repudiated sex; a dissolute gambler who became religious; an aristocrat who renounced his title; a writer struggling to fictionalize his observations of human nature who then rejected his own hard-won masterpieces. He could be disagreeable and rude or the kindest, gentlest of men.

His powerful intellect, expressed through a strong, charismatic personality, drew hundreds, then thousands of admirers and followers, a few of them photographers. Over the years a dozen or so amateurs and professionals spent time at the Tolstoy estate, cameras in hand, trying to catch the great man on film. As time passed the number of photographers increased. Sonya usually facilitated their efforts.

Some photographers who gained access to Tolstoy were followers of his social doctrines repudiating institutional religion and the autocracy; others were art lovers who appreciated his literary accomplishments; still others were friends or relatives. Occasionally, a professional photographer like Sergei Prokudin-Gorsky was called in for a special occasion or to illustrate an upcoming book.

The person who photographed Tolstoy most, apart from Sonya, was Vladimir Grigoryevich Chertkov. Chertkov, from a wealthy and prominent Russian family, met Tolstoy in 1883 when he was 29 years old and Tolstoy 55. He became Tolstoy's most ardent follower.

He began to photograph Tolstoy in 1905. On July 3rd that summer, he wrote to Sonya from England about one of his early photographic efforts: "I'm very sorry that almost all the photographs I shot from a short distance have been inadequate, partly perhaps because of my inexperience and partly because of inadequate film....But a few landscapes are just wonderful, with Lev Nikolaevich on foot or mounted amidst the local meadows and forests he loves so dearly. These photographs must please you because they are new as well as good."

By 1907 Chertkov was successfully making closeup portraits and had taken on the mission of photographing Tolstoy for posterity. Within a year he was building a house a few miles from Tolstoy's estate. He installed a photographic laboratory on the first floor, purchased fancy foreign cameras,

SOPHIA TOLSTOY: STUDY, YASNAYA POLYANA, NOVEMBER 3, 1903

SOPHIA TOLSTOY: YASNAYA POLYANA, MARCH 3, 1903

THOMAS TAPSELL: VLADIMIR CHERTKOV PHOTOGRAPHING TOLSTOY WITH MAIL, KOCHETY ESTATE, 1910

and hired a professional assistant photographer, an Englishman named Thomas Tapsell.

Tapsell worked alongside Chertkov photographing Tolstoy. He developed and printed Chertkov's pictures and also his own. There is no way to distinguish definitively between Chertkov's and Tapsell's photographs, but Chertkov expert Olga Yevgenyevna Yershova speculates that closeups are by Chertkov and everything else is by Tapsell. Tapsell's work was technically competent but that didn't improve Tolstoy's attitude as a subject. In a May 1910 letter to his youngest daughter Alexandra he wrote, "Chertkov is about to invite Tapsell. I'm not entirely pleased with it, but I cannot refuse Chertkov anything, and besides Tanya [Tolstoy's oldest daughter] likes it, so I like it too."

By his last years Tolstoy had developed an unshakable trust in Chertkov, who could intuit his moods, flatter and raise his spirits, and be present with a camera in his solitary moments and during encounters with peasants, though the camera had to be hidden in such circumstances. In a 1909 diary entry, Tolstoy wrote, "Chertkov was making my portraits. Did not interfere with my writing."

Insofar as they are documents of Tolstoy's life, Chertkov's photographs can be seen to complement Sonya's, hers emphasizing family and home life, his documenting social and missionary activities. Both tried to record Tolstoy's likeness and personality, Chertkov beginning 20 years after Sonya.

Gradually, Sonya and Chertkov grew to loathe one another. Chertkov sought to control all Tolstoy's writings. Sonya fought with him publicly and emotionally over Tolstoy's diaries and the rights to his literary work for posterity.

SERGEI PROKUDIN-GORSKY: YASNAYA POLYANA, MARCH 23, 1908

LEV TOLSTOY IN HIS STUDY, YASNAYA POLYANA, NOVEMBER 3, 1903 (BOTH)

SONYA AND LEV TOLSTOY were happiest during the early years of their marriage when he was writing his greatest novels. He wrote *War and Peace* in fits and starts, sometimes with long dry periods, which he described in his diary.

DIARY ENTRY (LEV) **16 September 1864**
It will soon be a year that I have written nothing on this book. Yet it has been a good year. The relations between Sonya and me have grown finer, stronger. We love, that is to say we are dearer to each other than to anyone else in the world, and we look at each other with clear eyes. We have no secrets and no cause for remorse.

Sonya was ever conscious of her husband's genius and devoted herself to serving it. Working at night, the only free time she had, she copied *War and Peace* in clear, flowing handwriting, leaving a large margin on one side of the paper for his corrections, sure to come. She copied *War and Peace* approximately seven times. Tolstoy recognized his wife's talent as a critic and diarist. He didn't often admit it but he took advantage of it, and Sonya was pleased.

DIARY ENTRY **12 November 1866**
...I now spend most of my time copying out Lyova's novel (which I am reading for the first time). This gives me great pleasure. As I copy I experience a whole new world of emotions, thoughts and impressions. Nothing touches me so deeply as his ideas, his genius. This has only been so recently. Whether it is because I have changed or because this novel really is extraordinarily good, I do not know. I write very quickly, so I can follow the story and catch the mood, but slowly enough to be able to stop, reflect upon each new idea and discuss it with him later. He and I often talk about the novel together, and for some reason he listens to what I have to say (which makes me very proud) and trusts my opinions.

The fifth volume of *War and Peace* was finally finished in 1869. On February 24, 1870, Sonya wrote a note for her future autobiography:
Yesterday he told me that he had in mind a type of woman who is married, in high society, but who ruins herself. He said that his problem was to make this woman only pitiful and not guilty, and as soon as he found her type, then all the other characters and male types he had thought of earlier fell into place and grouped themselves around this woman.

But Tolstoy, though he went so far as to draft an outline, didn't immediately begin this new project and instead immersed himself in researching Peter the Great, a book he later abandoned. Almost two years afterward, on January 18, 1872, Sonya wrote a letter to her sister Tanya about Anna Pirogova, a woman who was living with a Tolstoy neighbor:
...we had another dramatic incident here in Yasnaya. You remember Anna Stepanova over at Bibikov's—. Well, she was jealous of all the governesses....She threw herself under a train and was crushed to death.

Another 14 months passed before Sonya recorded that her husband had written a page and a half toward a new novel set in their own time, and he thought it good. Thus began *Anna Karenina.*

Sonya copied and recopied *Anna Karenina*, as she had done *War and Peace*, at night while the household slept. Sometimes she finished at 3 a.m., at which time she took the fresh pages to

Tolstoy's study and put them on his desk, ready for him to begin reworking in the morning.

Tolstoy struggled with *Anna Karenina* and wrote fitfully. Evidence of his groping and Sonya's devotion can be seen in the crossings-out and rewriting on every manuscript page. Even the novel's famous first line—*All happy families are alike; each unhappy family is unhappy in its own way*—didn't come easily.

As he worked, Tolstoy was plagued by doubt; during the four years he spent developing his layered story of betrayal and love, with all its complicated characters and intricate social issues, he frequently feared his text was tedious and pointless. But Sonya was enthralled as she saw the work unfold. In a letter to her sister Tanya dated December 9, 1876, she wrote:

We are now really at work on Anna Karenina, *that is, writing without interruption. Lyovochka is in a lively, concentrated state of mind; he adds a whole chapter each day. I work hard on the copying and already, lying under this very letter, I have the fresh copies of the new chapter he wrote yesterday.*

Tolstoy finished the novel in 1877 and was glad to be done with it. Royalty payments flowed in immediately and for the time being this alleviated the family's nagging financial problems (which stemmed from mismanagement and losses before Sonya entered the picture). But Tolstoy was already in the process of turning away from literature. He was taken up with religious questions, and he began to devote himself to writing religious tracts.

In November 1879, when he had been away from fiction writing for about two years, Sonya wrote her sister Tanya:

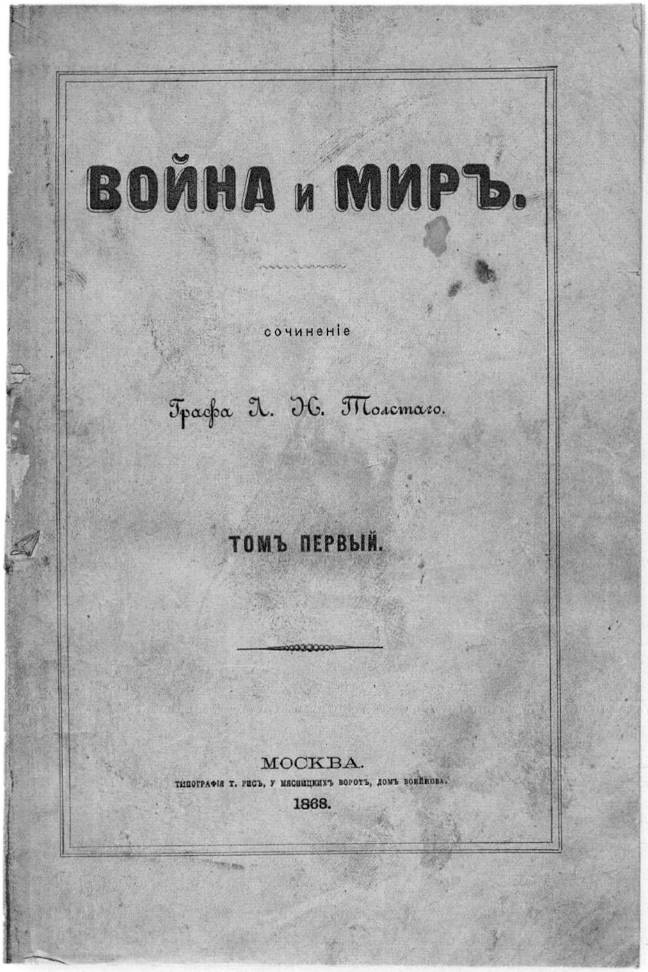

WAR AND PEACE, FIRST EDITION COVER, 1868

It's not the money I regret. There is something lacking in my life, something that I loved, and that is Lyova's literary work, which had always given me such joy and inspired me with such reverence. You see, Tanya, I'm a true writer's wife, so greatly do I take his writing to heart.

By 1882 Tolstoy had arrived at the belief that private property was immoral, and the idea grew in his mind to relinquish all copyrights to his literary work. He wanted to forego future royalties, to transfer copyright to the people. But Sonya did not support him. They clashed bitterly because Tolstoy's beliefs called for relinquishing the only way of life Sonya knew and valued.

The family's financial troubles had returned. Now the money did matter to Sonya. She took on the business of publishing and distributing the most lucrative works, and the revenue thus generated became the family's primary source of income. She proposed that her husband assign her the rights to the two works published before 1881, *War and Peace* and *Anna Karenina*. Tolstoy refused and they argued fiercely, but Sonya didn't give in. Finally in 1891, with most of the children supporting Sonya, Tolstoy reluctantly, painfully, agreed to what she wanted.

Through the years Sonya had a hand in publishing subsequent editions of *Anna Karenina*, and she continued to be taken up with the unforgettable character of Anna. She recorded her fresh thoughts 26 years after the novel was originally published, while working on a new edition to be published that year:

DIARY ENTRY **6 March 1903**

I have finished the proofs of Anna Karenina. *By following the state of her soul, step by step, I grew to understand myself and was terrified...But people do not take their lives to avenge themselves on someone; no, they take their lives because they* no longer *have the strength to live....At first it is struggle, then prayer, then reconciliation, then despair—and finally powerlessness and death....*

The couple's youngest daughter, Alexandra, wrote in her biography of Tolstoy published in 1953:

All during her life my mother meticulously saved the rough drafts of my father's writings; she never threw away a scrap of paper written on by him. The manuscripts of War and Peace *were laid aside in an unused room in the house at Yasnaya Polyana and for many years no one touched them....In time she had* 12 *wooden cases made, in which she put, in no particular order, all the Tolstoy manuscripts and sent them for safekeeping to the Rumyantsev Museum in Moscow.*

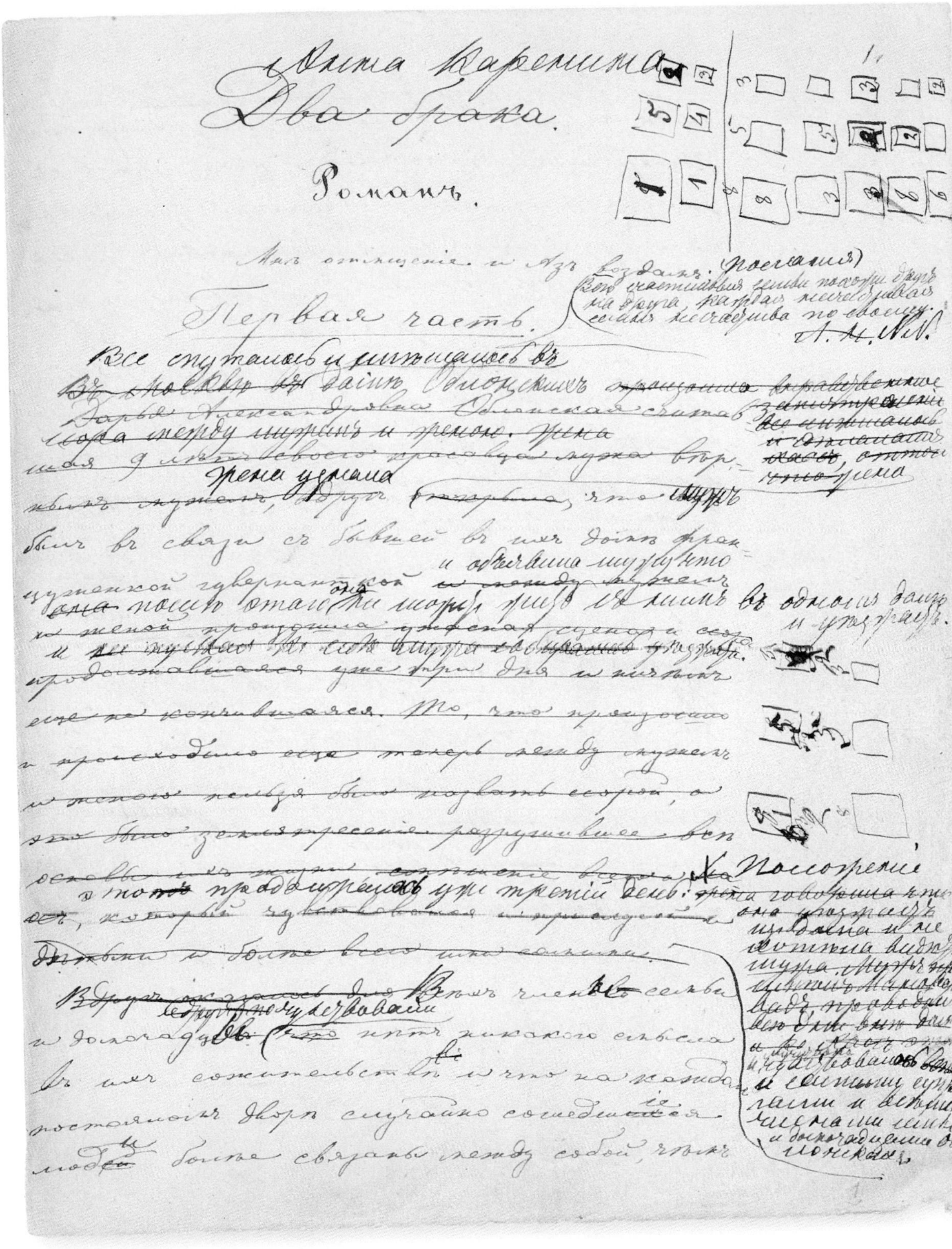

Анна Каренина

Два брака.

Романъ.

Мнѣ отмщеніе и Азъ воздамъ.

Первая часть.

ANNA KARENINA, FIRST PAGE, CIRCA 1873

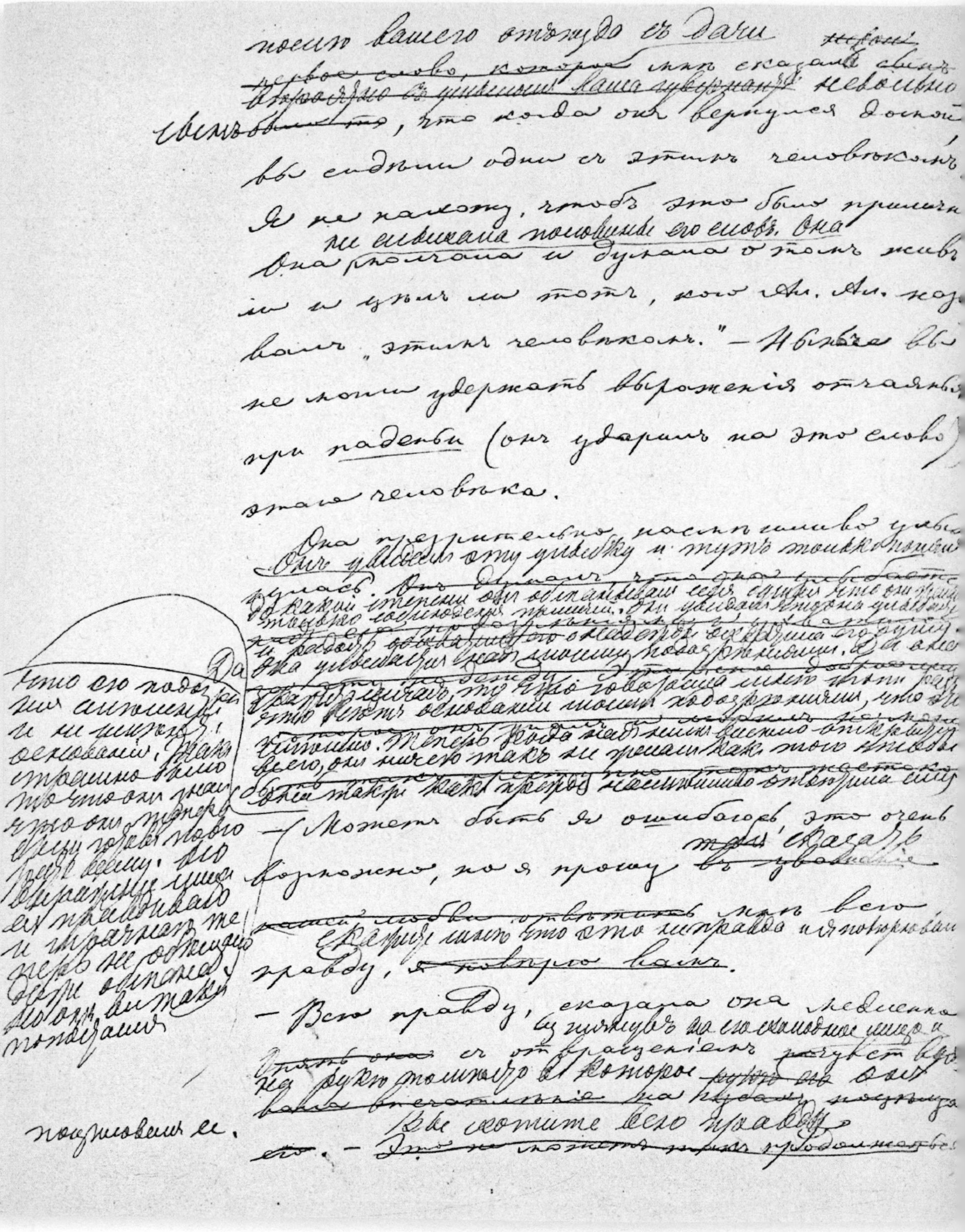
после вашего отъезда съ дачи
..., что когда онъ вернулся домой
вы сидѣли одни съ этимъ человѣкомъ
Я не помню, чтобъ это было причина
Она молчала и думала о томъ
называлъ „этимъ человѣкомъ."
не могли удержать выраженія отчаянія
при паденіи (онъ ударилъ на это слово)
этого человѣка.
— Можетъ быть я ошибаюсь, это очень
возможно, но я прошу
правду,
— Всю правду, сказала она
Вы хотите всю правду

ANNA KARENINA, READY FOR SONYA TO RECOPY

38 4.

хать. Я.
— Нет, я не буду, сказала Анна. — Я
Я так, только и
плачу от радости что видала тебя
О не буду, не буду, сказала она, утирая слезы и улыбаясь.
Ну тебе одеваться надо, сказала она
Теперь, сказала она [illegible] и оправившись и не выпуская
И Анна подняла его кровать на стул, на его руки, стала
котором было приготовлено платье его
[illegible], но не выпуская его руки.
— Как ты одеваешься без меня? Как
Как...
ты будешь молиться без меня. Сначала она начала говорить просто, но не могла
— Я не моюсь холодной водой, папа не велит. договорить и отвернулась.
А Василия Лукича ты не видала? Он
придет. А ты села на мое платье.
И Сережа Анна расхохотался. Она оглянулась на
него и [illegible] улыбалась, забыв утереть слезы.
— Мама, душечка, голубушка! закричал
он, бросаясь опять к ней и обнимая ее.
Как будто он теперь только ясно понял,
что случилось.
Это все какое
[illegible], говорил он [illegible] снимая
[illegible]
[illegible]
[illegible]
И как будто вновь увидав ее без шляпы, он опять бросился целовать ее;
[illegible] взглянул на нее
Да оно сказал
[illegible] Анна
[illegible] тихо нежно
[illegible] чтобы
[illegible] думали обо мне.
жить. [illegible] Ты и думать
[illegible] что [illegible]
[illegible] все [illegible] не [illegible]
[illegible] она хотела сказать: по
[illegible] трудно мой
мнишь меня, но [illegible]

IN THE SPRING OF 1859, Tolstoy opened a village school on his estate at Yasnaya Polyana. He was just emerging as a writer and may have been motivated in part by the knowledge that most Russians were illiterate and couldn't read what he published.

But more importantly he knew that literacy was crucial for improving the peasants' often desperate lot, a keen and growing interest of his. He was a wonderful teacher, energized by his success with his students. By the end of the first summer 20 children were attending classes.

His school continued to expand and he brought in assistant teachers. By the summer of 1860 he had decided he needed to learn more about educational practices in Germany, England, and elsewhere in Western Europe. He traveled for almost a year, visiting schools, talking with educators, and refining his opinions on teaching methods and curricula. He returned to Russia and to his school in the spring of 1861.

The children loved Tolstoy but local officials suspected that his ideas were dangerous. His conflicts with authorities on this and other matters seemed to fire his resolve. His dedication to literacy was lifelong.

Sonya made this picture of schoolchildren visiting Tolstoy from the nearby town of Tula in 1907. It is a record of the recognition Tolstoy was accorded, and is also Sonya's tribute to his work as an educator. Sonya chose it for one of her albums and it has been published in several biographies of Tolstoy.

TULA SCHOOLCHILDREN VISITING LEV TOLSTOY, 1907

TOLSTOY FAMILY, YASNAYA POLYANA, AUGUST 1887

The Family

"One thing I do find intolerably unjust...is the idea that one should have to renounce one's personal life in the name of universal love. I believe that there are obligations that are ordained by God, that no one has the right to deny them, and that the obligations actually promote rather than hinder the spiritual life."

6 March 1887

BETWEEN 1863 AND 1888 Sonya gave birth to 13 children. Eight lived to adulthood. Here are those eight, grouped around Sonya in a photograph she took at a friend's Crimean estate in 1902. The family had traveled there to be near Tolstoy while he convalesced from an illness Sonya described in her diary as "a disorder of the intestines, liver and stomach, and complete atony."

Petya was the first of Sonya's babies to die. He was her sixth child, born when Sergei, her oldest, was ten. She took up her diary to record the tragedy:

DIARY ENTRY **11 November 1873**

On November 9 at nine in the morning, my little Petyushka died of a throat infection. He died peacefully, after two days' illness. He was born on June 13th 1872, and I had fed him for fourteen and a half months. What a bright, happy little boy—I loved my darling too much and now there is nothing. He was buried yesterday. I cannot reconcile the two Petyas, the living and the dead; they are both precious to me, but what does the living Petya, so bright and affectionate, have in common with the dead one, so cold and still and serious....

Thoughts of death shadowed her for months afterward. She made only one diary entry in 1874:

DIARY ENTRY **February 17, 1874**

When I think of the future I see a blank. I am haunted by the gloomy premonition that as soon as the grass grows over Petya's grave they will have to plough it up for me.

During that mournful year Sonya considered the fact that pregnancy could be averted. She was pregnant with her seventh child while she was still recovering from the death of Petya. Anna Pirogova, the very neighbor who later threw herself under a train and thereby became a model for Tolstoy's heroine Anna Karenina, had recently explained the practice of contraception to Sonya, saying she didn't want any children to come from her affair with Alexander Bibikov, even if they were to get married.

At first Sonya was horrified at the thought of it. The very idea that by her own hand her existing children would not be alive seemed unthinkable and the height of interference with God and nature. But the idea, once planted, didn't go away and she began to wish for the relief contraception could provide and proposed it to her husband. But he wouldn't hear of it.

By the 12th pregnancy she was desperate. She decided on abortion, first appealing for help from a midwife, who, not wanting to get involved in this controversial undertaking with Tolstoy's wife, turned her down. Then she took hot baths, and finally she jumped off a chest of drawers in her room. But on June 19, 1884, she gave birth to a healthy baby girl, who was named Alexandra and called Sasha.

Tolstoy had strong views on matters of bringing children into the world and nurturing them. In addition to opposing contraception he was against hiring a wet nurse, though most women of Sonya's class hired one with the birth of each baby. Sonya was willing to do what her husband wished but right away she had problems nursing her first child Sergei. She didn't give up easily, but her repeated efforts were increasingly painful. Even when her breasts grew inflamed, Tolstoy wouldn't allow her to bring in a wet

SONYA WITH HER EIGHT SURVIVING CHILDREN, GASPRA ESTATE, CRIMEA, 1902

nurse, but then open sores developed and Sonya's mother and others in the household insisted that complying with Tolstoy's demands in this matter would lead to a grave infection. A doctor was called. Tolstoy relented with reluctance and Sonya worried that she'd lose his love.

Lev Tolstoy's ideas about motherhood arose from his first major loss in life, the death of his own mother when he was two years old. The tales he heard during childhood about his mother and his acute sense of her absence shaped his unrealistic, idealistic view of what a mother could be. In his 1851 book titled Childhood, written when he was 23, he portrayed the mother as a faraway, yearned-for image. More than a half century later, at the age of 80, he wrote:

This morning I was strolling round the garden and as always I recalled Mother, "mommy," whom I do not remember at all but who has remained for me the holy ideal. I have never heard a bad thing about her. While walking through the birch groves, as I was approaching the grove of nut trees, I saw in the mud the imprint of a woman's foot and thought of her, her body. But I could not imagine it. Everything bodily would defile her....

THOUGH SONYA GREW EXHAUSTED from childbearing and wanted the pregnancies to stop, she loved each child richly once he or she was born. She rejoiced in her children's strengths, worried over their weaknesses, fussed over every illness, and deliberated endlessly over their upbringing and emotional life. She noted daily incidents and observations in her diary.

DIARY ENTRY **3 March 1887**

Masha is ill and I have been reading King Lear to her. I love Shakespeare, even though he sometimes does not know where to draw the line—witness all those brutal murders and innumerable deaths.

DIARY ENTRY **28 December 1890**

...When I look at my son Lyova I see a person of such intelligence, experience and talent, yet so little sense of self-protection: everything interests, excites, agitates and torments him.

DIARY ENTRY **16 February 1891**

....I gave the children a music lesson; we are progressing slowly but progressing none the less. Andryusha is playing a Beethoven sonata and Misha one of Haydn's. Misha is incomparably more gifted.

DIARY ENTRY **12 February 1901**

All the children were ill today, with various ailments: Tanya and Masha have stomach-aches, Misha has a toothache, Vanechka has a rash and Andryusha has a fever and has been vomiting.

Sonya took charge of her children's education and spent winters in Moscow or St. Petersburg with the older ones when she felt they could benefit from the educational resources those cities had to offer. At home she involved herself with the lessons of the younger children. She dealt with Sasha, the child she had tried to abort, the way she did the others.

DIARY ENTRY **14 June 1897**

I worked hard with Sasha all morning. I corrected her English translation and her essay, entitled 'Domestic Animals,' then I asked her to repeat her geography lesson on China. She is a quick, attentive student, and never gives me any trouble. I love teaching, and am used to doing it now....

DIARY ENTRY **15 July 1897**

I got up late, developed some prints, then went swimming with Sasha and the governesses. Afterwards I did some more developing and gave Sasha her lesson, which went very well today; I set her an essay to write on 'The Forest,' and we read various extracts from Turgenev and others who have described the forest. I pointed out to her that the beauty of these writers' descriptions lay in the detail, in personal impressions rather than artistic imagination. She appeared to understand perfectly. I then corrected her English translation—a story about the ancient philosophers—and asked her questions on the geography of America.

Tolstoy was devoted to his children but indifferent to the kind of education Sonya wanted for them. He hoped his offspring would follow in his footsteps and embrace his mission to transform society by fighting economic and social injustice. In a diary entry dated June 12, 1898, he wrote, "The sight of my children owning land and making the people work has such a strange and depressing effect on me. Like pangs of conscience. And this is not a reasoned judgment, but a feeling, and a very strong one. Was I wrong not to have given my land to the peasants? I don't know."

Sonya declared that, "all the things he preaches for the happiness of humanity only complicate life to the point where it becomes harder and harder for me to live." She felt strongly about her educational philosophy and guilty toward the children.

DIARY ENTRY **26 October 1886**

...I think a lot about the older boys—it grieves me that they have grown so distant. Why do fathers not grieve for their children? Why is it only women whose lives are burdened this way?

DIARY ENTRY **2 December 1901**

....Last night I wrote letters to our four absent sons, and was then kept awake all night by a mass of tormenting memories of my children's early years, my passionate anxious relationships with them, the unwitting mistakes I made in their education and my relationship with them now they are grown up. Then my thoughts turned to my dead children. I saw with astonishing clarity first Alyosha, then Vanechka, at various moments of their lives. I had a particularly vivid vision of Vanechka, thin and ill in bed, when after his prayers, which he almost invariably said in my presence, he would curl up into a cozy little ball and go off to sleep. I remember how it broke my heart to see his little back and to feel his tiny bones under my hand....

FIVE TOLSTOY BROTHERS: LEV, ILYA, SERGEI, ANDREI, AND MIKHAIL, YASNAYA POLYANA, AUGUST 1904

SONYA WITH DAUGHTER TANYA, YASNAYA POLYANA, JULY 1897

SONYA WITH SONS ANDREI (ANDRYUSHA) AND MIKHAIL (MISHA)
AND THEIR FRIEND BUTENOV (IN CENTER), YASNAYA POLYANA, JULY 1898

SONYA'S TWO BEST FRIENDS were her sister Tanya and her daughter Tanya. In this 1898 photograph of her profile with theirs, she placed her sister in the middle and her daughter in front for visual balance.

Sonya also had sisterly feelings toward others in her extended family. Her capacity for devotion and friendship led to easy bonds, even across generations, with women like her nieces Liza and Vera, mentioned in this diary entry:

DIARY ENTRY **29 September 1897**

...This evening we...went out onto the balcony—it was a heavenly moonlit night, warm, with a south wind and small transparent clouds racing across the moon, now veiling, now revealing it. Tanya, Liza Obolenskaya, Vera and I sat up late sewing, foolishly telling each others' fortunes with cards and chatting about intimate matters. Women can be open with one another about everything—one can only be weak and unguarded with people one has loved since childhood, when one knows every detail of their character, every event of their life. I am closer to my sister Tanya than to anyone else.

But Sonya's relations with her own daughters were mixed and complex. Sasha, the youngest, grew to hate her mother, thinking she was the cause of all her father's problems. This may have been, in part, because Sasha came of age when her parents were openly estranged and when Vladimir Chertkov was a divisive force in the household; she saw this fraught side of her family's life far more than the older children did.

When the Russian Revolution and World War I were over, Sasha moved to the United States where she established the Tolstoy Foundation in Valley Cottage, New York. She spent the rest of her life working on behalf of Tolstoyan causes in health and education and writing about her father. In her 1953 book titled, *Tolstoy: A Life of My Father*, she described her sister, Tanya:

Tanya was not beautiful; She was attractive. She had a wonderful complexion, brilliant dark-brown eyes, a short, sharply chiseled pert little nose, wavy chestnut hair, a slim, graceful figure and with them talent, wit and a buoyant charm. She was pleasing to old and young. In social circles she enchanted everyone with her tact, her ability to handle herself, her wit and gaiety; simple people were attracted to her by her goodness and unaffected manners.

Though Sonya felt photography was inadequate to register a person's true beauty, she photographed her children and their spouses and families until she grew old, Tolstoy died, Russia changed, and the family broke up.

DAUGHTER TANYA, SISTER TANYA, AND SONYA, YASNAYA POLYANA, 1903

SON ILYA WITH HIS FAMILY, MANSUROVO ESTATE, CIRCA 1905

ILYA'S CHILDREN ANNOCHKA, ILYSHOK, AND VOLODYA, YASNAYA POLYANA, 1903

SONYA AND LEV TOLSTOY WITH SONYA'S SISTER TANYA, DAUGHTER TANYA IN GREENERY, YASNAYA POLYANA, AUGUST 1898 (BOTH)

SONYA AND LEV TOLSTOY WITH SON MISHA IN GREENERY, YASNAYA POLYANA, AUGUST 1898

SONYA OCCASIONALLY TOOK the time to experiment with compositional ideas. She managed to be simultaneously serious and playful, and obviously enjoyed herself. In August 1898 she photographed herself with her husband, sister, daughter, and son variously arranged on the porch at the back of their house.

Misha, her tenth child, peering through the bushes at right in the horizontal version of this composition, had himself recently begun photographing, a fact Sonya noted with pleasure in three separate diary entries that same August.

By then she had begun to have grandchildren. Photographing them was an act of love; she took pictures of them individually, in twos and threes, with Lev, and with herself.

SONYA WITH GRANDSON LYOVUSHKA, YASNAYA POLYANA, 1898

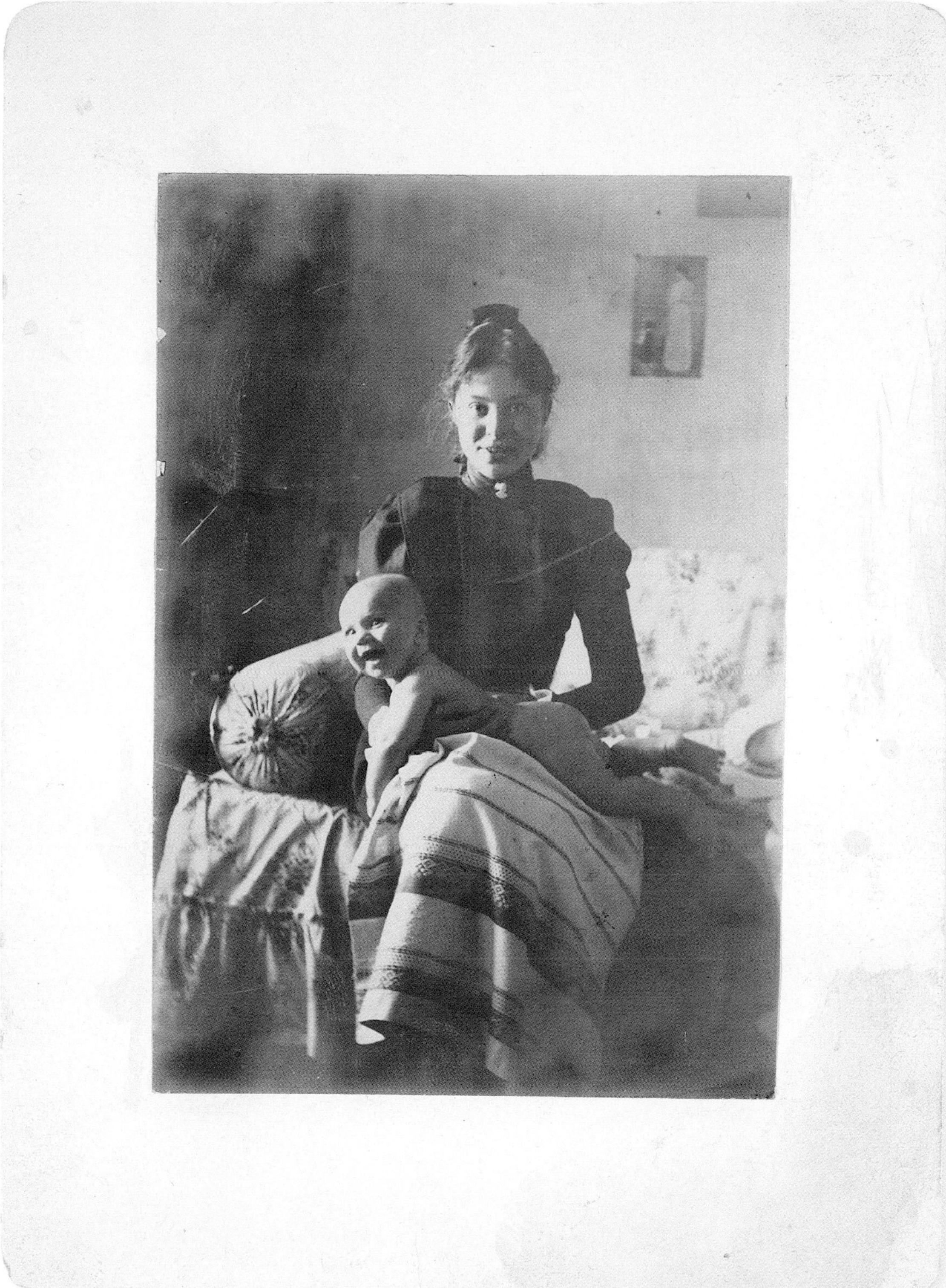

DAUGHTER-IN-LAW DORA (WIFE OF SON LEV) WITH HER SON LYOVA, YASNAYA POLYANA, 1899

SONYA WITH HER GRANDCHILDREN SONECHKA (IN HER ARMS) AND LYOVUSHKA, YASNAYA POLYANA, 1900

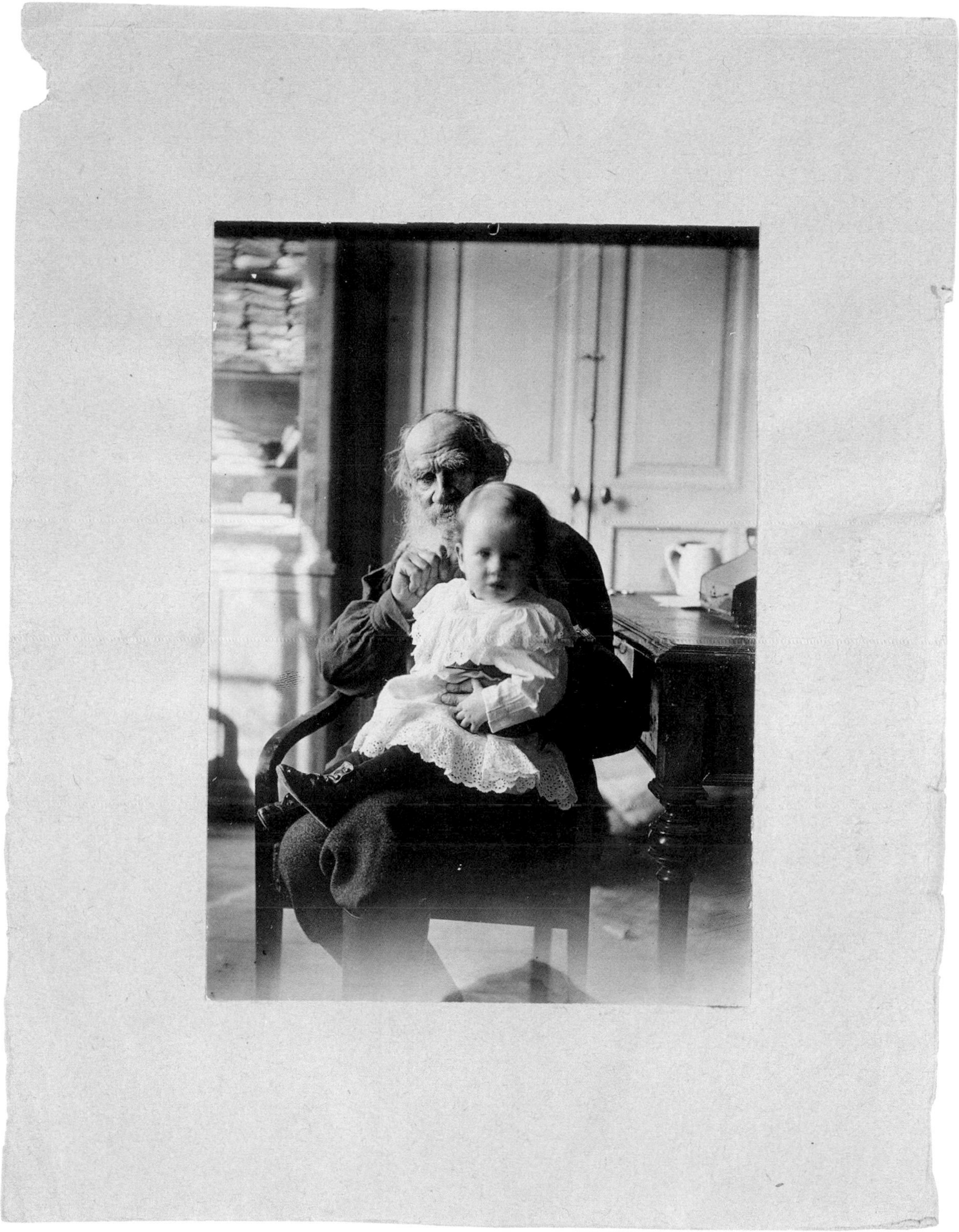

TOLSTOY WITH GRANDDAUGHTER TANECHKA, YASNAYA POLYANA, MAY 1907

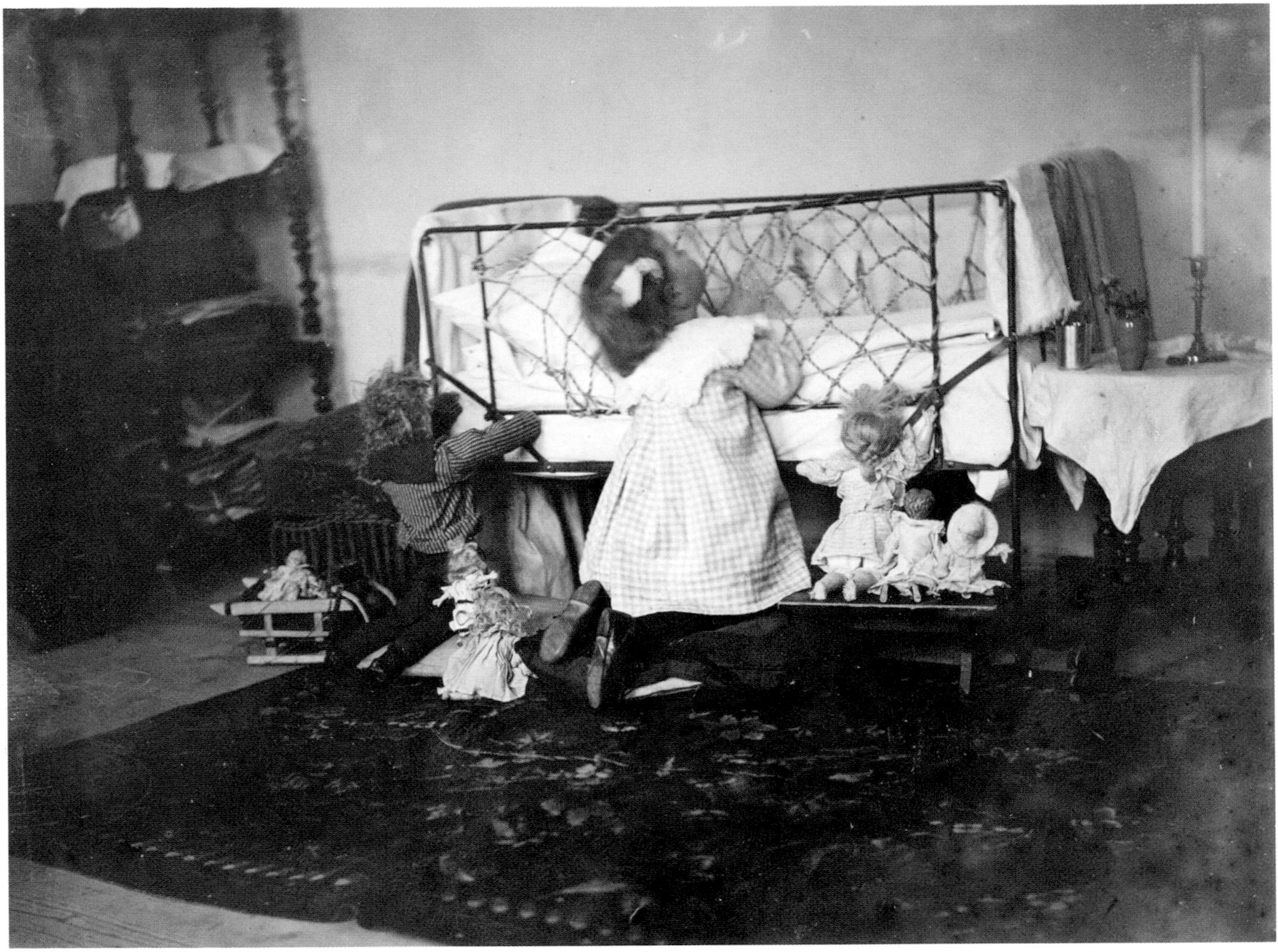

GRANDDAUGHTER TANECHKA SUKHOTINA AT PRAYER WITH DOLLS, YASNAYA POLYANA, 1908

GRANDDAUGHTER TANECHKA WITH DOLLS, YASNAYA POLYANA, 1908

MISHA'S SON VANECHKA WITH HIS SISTER TANECHKA, YASNAYA POLYANA, CIRCA 1904

GRANDSON SERGEI, SERYOZHA'S SON FROM HIS FIRST MARRIAGE, YASNAYA POLYANA

ILLUSTRATION FOR SONYA'S CHILDREN'S STORY "*SKELETON DOLLS*," CIRCA 1905

IN ADDITION TO DUTIFULLY educating her children, Sonya devoted herself to amusing them. She had parties on Christmases and birthdays and fabricated games and stories for ordinary days. She was serious about her stories, illustrating them with photographs and saving them. In 1910 Sonya wrote a children's story called "Skeleton Dolls." (Skeleton dolls were figures made for dressing up, like paper dolls.) She made a photograph to accompany the text. The story was published in her book titled, *Skeleton Dolls and Other Stories.*

Sonya wrote"Granny's Treasure" in 1893. Two years later it was published in the magazine *Childhood Reading*, issue no. 12. Here is a short summary:

GRANNY'S TREASURE

LEGEND

I.

In 1812, there was a war between the Russians and the French. The French army entered Russia, reached Moscow, and began to burn the city. Many inhabitants fled. But one rich landowner's widow by the name of Yelizaveta Fyodorovna Glebova decided to stay in her opulent mansion near Moscow in the village of Yelyizavetyno where she lived with her ten-year-old grandson, Fedya. Everybody warned her that the French would kill her if she stayed, but she was too old and sick to travel.

Finally she realized she had to go, but first she had a job to do: She got out of bed in the middle of the night, lugged a large trunk into the middle of her room and, with the help of her faithful maid, filled the trunk with gold, precious stones, and silver crockery. Her coachman and yard-keeper were summoned, and they heaved the heavy trunk onto a cart. Then Yelizaveta roused Fedya and off they went. The party drove a short distance from the house to an old oak tree near the edge of the forest, and with difficulty buried the treasure. As they were returning to the house, a Russian colonel and his men, worrying and searching for Yelizaveta, caught up with her. They gathered food and a few necessities and left for a safe refuge.

II.

Yelizaveta soon fell ill. On her deathbed she called her grandson Fedya and said to him, "I ask you not to dig up the treasure until you need it for some good deed. If you dig it up out of greediness it won't bring you happiness."

Years later, when Fedya finished school, he moved back to Yelizavetyno. The old house was empty and neglected. Fedya renovated it, became a businessman, and grew wealthy. But he was very lonely and his heart hardened from his loneliness.

Nikita, the coachman who had helped bury the treasure, was now old and was the only person left besides Fedya who remembered burying it. In a moment of weakness Nikita went to the oak tree and began to dig up the treasure chest. But when he pulled on the lock he was suddenly overcome with remorse and fear. He ran from the oak tree, soon lost his mind, left the estate, and went into a monastery.

III.

Now Fedya, who had been a kind-hearted boy, was a changed person. Over the years he had grown more greedy and lonely. He decided that the opportunity to do a good deed his grandmother had spoken of would never come. Better he should have the money and become even richer than let it lie in the ground and be of no use. He was tormented by this thought and finally decided to act on it. He purchased a shovel, went to the oak tree in the middle of the night and dug until he was exhausted. Suddenly an invisible force knocked him over. His feet were numb and he couldn't move. He didn't want to be found near the treasure so he pulled himself along on his hands, dragging his sick feet with difficulty until he reached a road.

At five in the morning a water bearer passed. Fedya was brought home and put in bed. Doctors came from far and wide but none could help. Fedya was confined to a wheelchair. He was wretched and helpless. He lost his business, the estate was dilapidated, and he became poor, but he was afraid to touch the treasure and didn't even consider it.

One summer night he was awakened by cries of "Fire!" Flames in the village were approaching his house. His servant, having run to the village to help relatives, didn't answer his calls. He was terrified and began to wrestle with God. Suddenly, even as his own house caught fire, he began to grieve over the misfortune of others. Fearing death he prayed, promising God that if he were spared he would devote his life to goodness. Just then his servant broke the window and saved him.

The next day Fedya asked to be taken to see the destroyed village. Everything had been lost in the fire. He cried together with people he had known from childhood and had not seen since. Now Fedya remembered the treasure and his heart leapt with joy. He showed the peasants the site and gave them all the money. They first built a new house for Fedya, then rebuilt the village. Fedya remembered his promise to God and lived in friendship and happiness with the villagers for the rest of his life. THE END

Sonya, like her husband, looked for a higher purpose in life. They assumed that fulfilling a purpose endows life with meaning. For some people, such a desire is easily gratified. For others, it can grow into a drive that's impossible to satisfy. It may be sharply focused from childhood, or a vague yearning that accompanies an individual through life. For Sonya this drive for purpose flared up as a girl. It subsided and was subsumed by falling in love, having children, and the wish, then duty, to serve her husband's work. But then it rose up again. It never stayed quiet for long.

DIARY ENTRY **19 January 1891**

...Almost in my sleep I taught the children music for two hours and corrected the proofs for The Kreutzer Sonata. *I don't know how I manage to work so hard and for so long! What a pity I have been unable to direct it toward something worthier and more elevated than this mechanical drudgery. If only I could write stories or draw pictures, how happy I would be...*

ILLUSTRATION FOR SONYA'S CHILDREN'S STORY "*GRANNY'S TREASURE*," YASNAYA POLYANA, 1893/4

All the circumstances surrounding Sonya's life were inimical to the creative endeavors she envisioned for herself. Neither her husband nor society respected her work—or the work of any woman for that matter—and Sonya didn't have much confidence in her own creations. But despite this she couldn't seem to help communicating her feelings and thoughts through music, photography, painting, and writing. She kept track of her efforts. This diary entry probably refers to her novella Song Without Words:

DIARY ENTRY **24 October 1897**

...This evening I started on the first chapter of my story. I think it will be good. But who can I ask for an opinion on it? I would like to write and publish it without telling a soul.

In 1904 she wrote a short story titled "Groans." She used the pseudonym "A Tired Woman," and submitted it for publication. Her daughter Sasha referred to the story as a prose poem and recalled that it appeared in a collection titled, "Life For All."

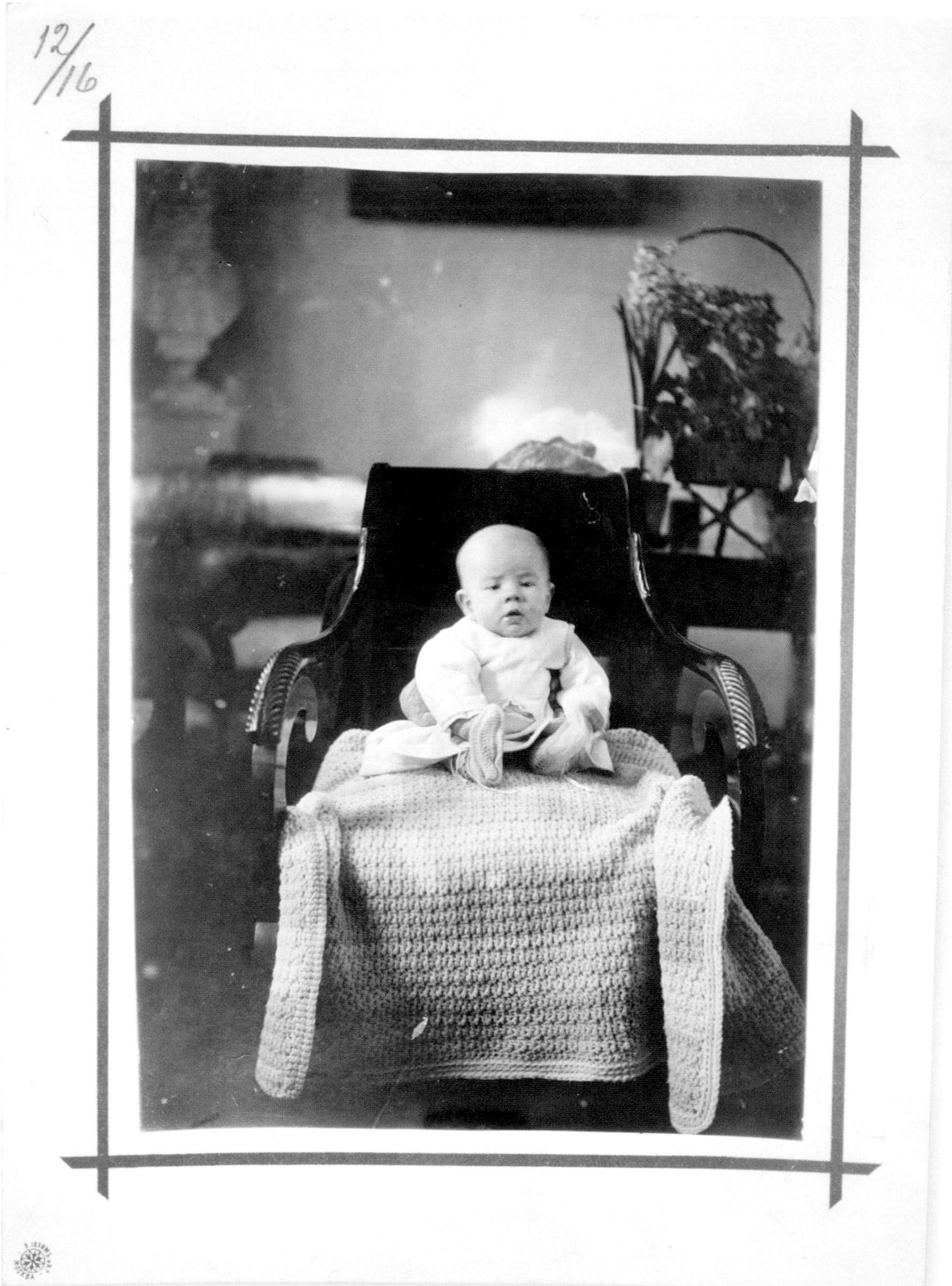

GRANDDAUGHTER TANECHKA SUKHOTINA, YASNAYA POLYANA, 1906

SONYA'S FAVORITE DAUGHTER, Tanya, finally gave birth to her own daughter after several failed pregnancies. Relieved and overjoyed, Tanya made a brief entry in the diary she had kept since age 13:

DIARY ENTRY (TANYA) **6 November 1905**
Today my own little Tatiana was born.

Sonya didn't record the event in her own diary, but of her 31 grandchildren this little girl held a special place in her heart. She entertained and photographed the child—variously called Tanya, Tanechka, and Tanyushka—and sent her this illustrated letter, not dated:

My dear granddaughter Tanyushka,

I am afraid you have quite forgotten your grandmother and those poor little pictures, which I would draw for you. We are looking forward to seeing you at Yasnaya Polyana and I again will be playing with my Tanyushka at a company of dollies, we'll be making a little garden, and little houses, and little bridges. There are already flowers with you in Rome, and we still have snow. Yesterday we went for a drive and Annochka fell out of the sledge twice. I kiss you and greet the nurse.

Grandmother.

Милая моя внучка
Танюшка,
Я боюсь, что ты
совсѣмъ забыла свою
бабушку и тѣ плохія
картиночки, которыя
я тебѣ рисовала.
Мы васъ ждемъ
въ Ясную Поляну,
и я буду опять
играть съ моей Та-
нюшкой въ компанію
куколокъ, будемъ дѣлать
садикъ, и домики, и
мостики. У васъ въ Римѣ
ужъ цвѣты, а у насъ все
снѣгъ. Вчера катались и
Анночка два раза вывалилась
изъ саней. Цѣлую тебя и
кланяюсь нянѣ. Бабушка.

LEV TOLSTOY WITH SONYA AND NIECES VERA AND LIZA, DAUGHTERS OF HIS SISTER MARIA, YASNAYA POLYANA, AUGUST 1901

Estate Life

"I am completely absorbed in estate matters. But it is possible for me only because it brings me into contact with nature and I can admire it to my heart's content...Today I went to the apple orchards, where forty peasants were clearing the moss, cutting away the dead wood and smearing the tree trunks with a compound of clay, lime and cow dung. What a beautiful sight the bright figures of the girls made against the background of the dazzling green grass, the blue sky and the yellow, red and brown trees."

30 September 1908

YASNAYA POLYANA, THE TOLSTOY ESTATE, 1897

WHENEVER THE 4,000-ACRE Tolstoy family estate, Yasnaya Polyana, was passed from one generation to the next it went to the youngest son. Accordingly, Lev Tolstoy inherited the title when family properties were divided in 1847: He was the youngest of the four then-eligible Tolstoy brothers—only a sister, Maria, was younger. He was 19, his novels and spiritual struggles still far in the future.

Yasnaya Polyana, translated as Clear Meadow, stretched pleasantly across a valley along the river Voronka, near the old town of Tula, about 120 miles south of Moscow. In Tolstoy's day it lay in view of a heavily traveled highway connecting Moscow to the south of Russia, to Kiev, the Caucasus, and the Crimea.

Tolstoy's maternal grandfather, Prince Nikolai Sergeyevich Volkonsky, was the first to build on the property. He started constructing parks, ponds, and buildings toward the end of the 18th century. The original house had two wings, 36 rooms, imposing columns, and a grand stairway. Tolstoy was born there on August 28, 1828. In 1860, when he was 32, he gambled away the central portion of the main house, and it was removed brick by brick. He was filled with self-loathing over this terrible outcome of his gambling addiction. When Sonya arrived only the two smallish wings were there, separated by a yard where the central part of the building had connected them. One of the wings was the school Tolstoy had established for peasant children; the other, slightly larger, was the couple's home.

Despite his youthful gambling habit, Tolstoy's attachment to Yasnaya Polyana was emotional and deep. He featured it in *War and Peace* as Lysiye Gory (Bald Hills), the beloved estate of Prince Bolkonsky. Near the end of his life, Tolstoy wrote that it would be difficult for him to imagine Russia and his relationship to it without Yasnaya Polyana. It was through his intimate knowledge of Yasnaya Polyana's geography and the way the seasons shaped it that he understood his homeland, and from his experience with the local peasantry he worried over Russia's destiny.

In 1891, 44 years after Tolstoy inherited Yasnaya Polyana, he decided to continue the tradition of passing the estate to the youngest son by willing the property to little Vanechka. But the transfer was never made; Vanechka died before he was seven. At the end of 1918, eight years after Tolstoy's death and the year before Sonya's, the estate was taken over by the Bolsheviks for use as a farm commune, but the buildings stayed intact. Sonya was allowed to stay there, and within a short time the government decided to preserve everything as it had been during Tolstoy's lifetime. For nearly a century now—through years of domestic turmoil and global catastrophe—the estate has been so perfectly kept that you can still feel Tolstoy's and Sonya's presence there.

When Sonya first arrived from Moscow at the age of 18, she found Yasnaya Polyana plainly furnished, mostly uncarpeted, populated with mice, and very quiet. She devoted herself to decorating the house and landscaping the neglected gardens, gradually turning the estate into a warm, comfortable, lively home. She entertained friends, relatives, and guests there and took pictures of it inside and out. She photographed the view opposite in 1897. By that time the wing that served as the main house, shown here at center, had been enlarged to accommodate the Tolstoys' ever-growing family.

ENTRANCE TO YASNAYA POLYANA, 1897

REAR OF THE HOUSE, SUMMER 1896

REMOVING SNOW FROM THE ROOF, YASNAYA POLYANA, 1908

THE LARGER POND WITH PINE TREES, YASNAYA POLYANA, 1897

SONYA KNITTING IN THE SALON AT YASNAYA POLYANA, 1902

A STILL PHOTOGRAPH CONNOTES stillness. This was more the case in Sonya's day than it is now. A sitter had to remain perfectly motionless while being photographed due to slow shutter speeds and also because of aesthetic preferences—a blurry subject or helter-skelter composition was evidence the photographer was unskilled. In all likelihood that outdated and unfashionable view contributes, in some small way at least, to a sense that life today is more frenetic than it used to be. The concussions of clashing elements, content spilling out over the edges of frames in much current photography, was all but absent in 19th- and early 20th-century photography.

This is a reason why Sonya's characteristic energy and constant busyness doesn't come through in her photographs. Sonya's in-born energy was fueled by a high-strung nature and constant agitation over the quality and intensity of her relationships, especially her volatile relationship with her husband. In 1902, the year she made this photograph, he was ill with typhus and recovering in its aftermath. His death was feared over and over again. Sonya nursed him day and night. She also kept up with her other tasks, and still made time for photography.

In this picture she wanted to show details of the salon at Yasnaya Polyana with herself casually but usefully occupied. Neatly arranging the chairs along a wall and around the table, attentive to framing, she included two windows at left and balanced the composition with two ancestral paintings on the wall and a small table topped with a bouquet of flowers placed behind her own seat. Her hands are clearly articulated against the dark chair and her black dress.

Not seen in this or other pictures is the fact that Sonya seemed constitutionally unable to remain idle—a trait that didn't go unobserved by her family. Her children and grandchildren repeatedly noted it in their diaries and memoirs.

Misha, her tenth child, wrote,

The amount of work my mother did wouldn't have been feasible even for a strong, healthy man. All day long she was busy teaching children, keeping household records, cutting and sewing bed linens and clothes for her children and husband; and after all that, her eyes sick with tiredness, she sat until two or three o'clock in the morning proofreading.

Sasha, her 12th child, wrote,

...Mama was busy all the time. When large quantities of books sent to Father by authors and publishers accumulated in our hall, Mama, with the help of Yulia Ivanovna or Abrikosov, who often came to stay in our house, piled them into cases, recorded them in a catalogue she had made, and arranged them on shelves. She collected clips from newspapers and glued them into special books. She photographed with enthusiasm and developed and printed the pictures herself.

Sometimes, not knowing what to do with her energy, Mama gathered litter, cigarette butts, scraps of paper, and burned all of it, despite the fact that we had a gardener and scores of daymen hanging about the house. She kept garden tools in her room: a small English shovel, a scythe with a whetstone, a rake, a hammer, nails, pruning shears, a saw. In summer, when nettles and burdock began to overtake the house, Mama mowed them clean. In autumn and in spring she cut out dead branches of lilac and acacia. She enjoyed painting garden tables, benches, a washstand in the house.

Mama had enormous energy. She couldn't remain

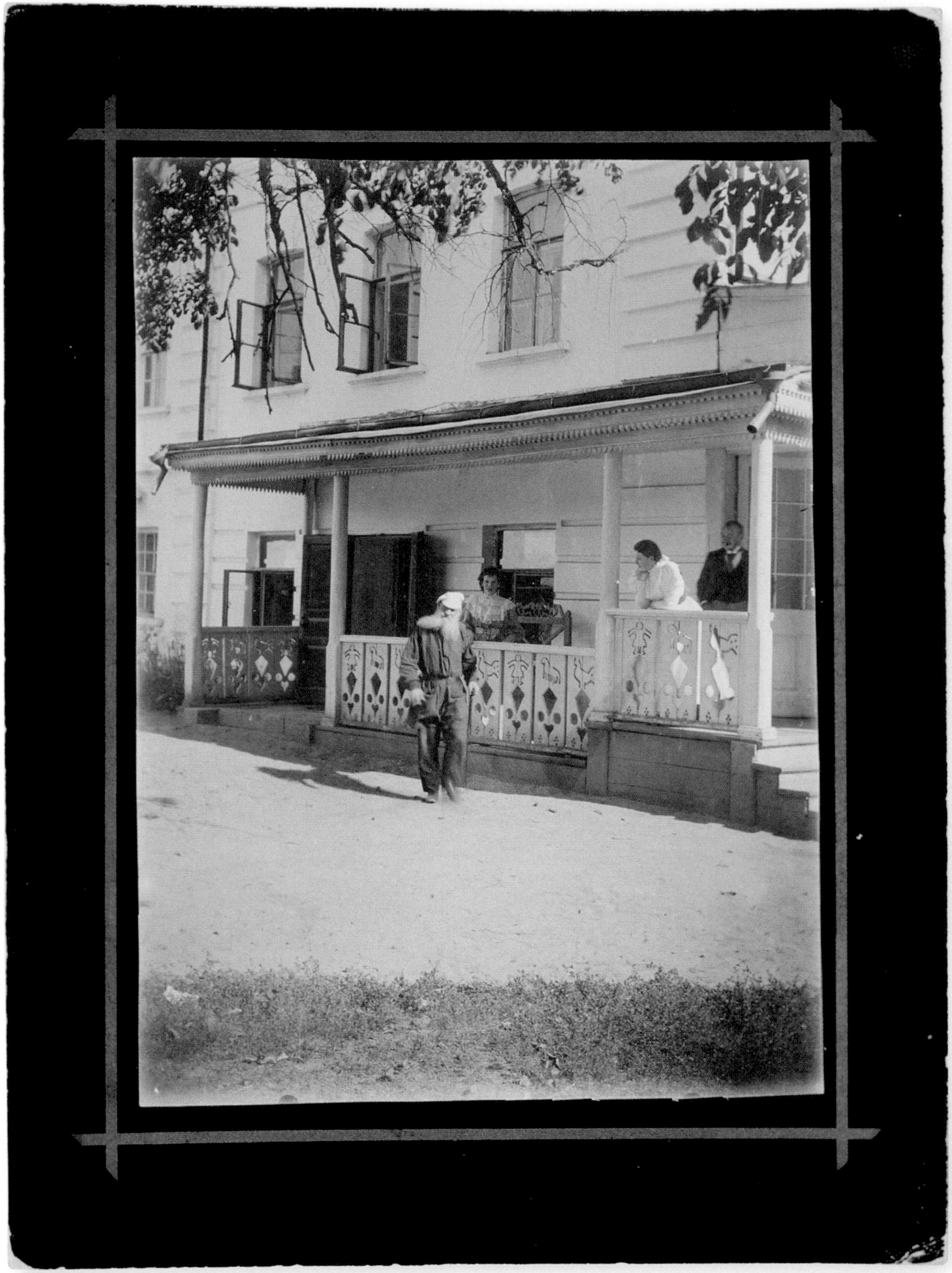

LEV TOLSTOY WITH HIS CHILDREN MARIA, SASHA, AND ANDREI, YASNAYA POLYANA, 1898

TOLSTOY WITH HIS DAUGHTER TANYA, YASNAYA POLYANA, JUNE 21, 1904

inactive. Once, for days on end, she studied typewriting. Also, unexpectedly, she took up painting, copied portraits of ancestors, of Father, and began to paint my portrait. Painting was replaced by writing. In "Life For All" a prose poem titled Goans appeared, the author of which was my mother. But music was above all her other passions.

Granddaughter Annochka, daughter of her third child Ilya, wrote in her memoirs,
She was always busy. In the morning she would record expenses, put things in order, try on her dresses, which were constantly sewn and made over. Having drunk plenty of coffee, she would begin playing piano scales, or run—it's impossible to say about her that she walked—with oil paints to sketch a pond, a garden path, mushrooms, herbs, flowerets, a house. Then she would write something—she made entries in her diary almost daily. Then she would put books in order. Then proofs would arrive…she would sit down in a living room next to Grandfather's study and get busy.

LEV TOLSTOY WITH RELATIVES AND GUESTS: TOLSTOY IS SPEAKING WITH S. SOLOMON, AUTHOR OF ARTICLES ON HIM AND TRANSLATOR OF HIS WORKS INTO FRENCH; TOLSTOY'S SISTER MARIA IS IN THE FOREGROUND; SONYA IS BUYING BERRIES FROM PEASANT GIRLS, YASNAYA POLYANA. JULY 15, 1899

LEV TOLSTOY WITH RELATIVES AND GUESTS: THIRD FROM LEFT, SEATED NEXT TO TOLSTOY, IS J. MAYOR, PROFESSOR OF POLITICAL ECONOMY FROM TORONTO; S. SOLOMON IS SEATED WITH A NEWSPAPER BESIDE SONYA, YASNAYA POLYANA, JULY, 1899

LEV TOLSTOY STROLLING IN THE APPLE ORCHARD WITH RELATIVES AND GUESTS, YASNAYA POLYANA, AUGUST 9, 1903

TOLSTOY WITH HIS SISTER MARIA NIKOLAEVNA, YASNAYA POLYANA, SEPTEMBER 1, 1898

SONYA AND LEV TOLSTOY WITH RELATIVES AND GUESTS, YASNAYA POLYANA, AUGUST 1896

SONYA'S PHOTOGRAPHS have an intimacy that gives a feel for what it was like to be there. You can practically smell the mud stuck to carriage wheels and feel the damp chill requiring a blanket over your knees at the start of a journey; you can sense the family's restlessness, waiting on the porch for guests to arrive; you can discern a sudden quiet descending on the table in the yard, a moment ago alive with talk, now suddenly stopped and held for the camera.

In part, it's the everyday minutiae, the commonplace gestures and postures that make the pictures familiar. And Sonya's seemingly artless approach, unencumbered by the era's photographic fashions, keeps much of her work from feeling dated. She photographed straight on, unpretentiously framing her characters to include the paraphernalia of their settings and giving them ample room to breathe. Her photographs are scenes from a soap opera—the true and very public story of her life with Lev Tolstoy.

When Sonya and her new husband began their life in his ancestral home, she was still in many ways a child, and a sheltered child at that. She cried the whole two days it took to get to Yasnaya Polyana. She could hardly bear to leave her family, she had no experience managing an estate, and she was afraid of Tolstoy's strong sexual desires.

She was greeted in her new home by Tolstoy's Aunt Toinette and other longtime members of the household, including Tolstoy's old nanny, his personal attendant, his grandmother's maid, a cook, a laundress, and other staff. The subdued atmosphere was a big change from the vibrant warmth of the home Sonya left, but brought up to be a good wife she took on the supervision of the housekeeping and began to manage the accounts. To please her husband she sewed jackets and trousers for him and, supported by the servants, she gardened and prepared food.

By spring the gardens bloomed and friends and family arrived for extended visits. There were picnics in April, evening hunts in May when the woodcocks were in flight; there was tennis, mushroom gathering, and swimming as spring turned to summer.

On June 28, 1863, nine months and five days after their wedding, Sonya gave birth to the Tolstoys' first son, Sergei. The marriage was off to a vigorous start. But the Tolstoys, both of them passionate and impetuous, were battling each other from the beginning. At first it was because they distrusted each other's love. (She thought he was in love with a peasant woman who had borne him a son and still worked in the house; he feared she found him old and unattractive.) In later years Tolstoy's ascetic beliefs, peasant habits, and the peasant followers he brought into their home, abhorrent to Sonya, led to greater, longer-lasting clashes.

But through all their years of discord the guests kept coming. Sonya kept a record of who came and went.

DIARY ENTRY **11March 1906**

Sergeyenko came with his daughter and read me some passages from his biography of Lev Nikolaevich, including various things about me. It's fairly accurate and not too bad...

Here Sonya was referring to writer Pyotr Alekseyevich Sergeyenko who was working on the second edition of his biography, *How L. N. Tolstoy Lives and Works*. The first edition had been published in Moscow in 1898. She must have liked this passage:

Sophia Andreyevna is an excellent hostess; attentive, polite, and hospitable. Dining and staying at Yasnaya Polyana is just like being at home.

The entire complex and painstaking job of running the household and attending to all matters is in the hands of Sophia Andreyevna. She is tireless in bringing her lively energy and domestic management skills to bear at every turn. It was no wonder that the coachman noted that the Countess was "wild about order." If other matters were to take her away from Yasnaya Polyana for even a day or two, the complicated mechanism known as a "household" would soon start to creak and run down.

SONYA AND LEV TOLSTOY WITH GUESTS AND CHILDREN—INCLUDING TANYA, SERGEI, ANDREI, MIKHAIL, AND SASHA—AT THE FRONT OF THE HOUSE IN THE PARK, YASNAYA POLYANA, AUGUST 4, 1899

TENNIS GAME: TOLSTOY WITH DAUGHTER SASHA AND OTHER RELATIVES, YASNAYA POLYANA, 1896

DIARY ENTRY 1 **September 1898**

...I went out with my camera and dashed about taking photographs of the park, my grandchildren, L. N. and his sister, the forest, the path to the swimming pool, and the charming Yasnaya countryside.

Sonya's photographs paint a better picture than her written diary of the pastimes and entertainments of family and guests. She kept scant notes on many of the specific daily activities at Yasnaya Polyana.

DIARY ENTRY 12 **February 1901**

...How can one keep things tidy when there are people constantly coming to visit and stay, and dragging yet more guests after them....crowds of people milling around from morning to night...

Several Tolstoy children kept diaries or wrote memoirs. Ilya, the third child and second son, finished writing his reminiscences when he was 67, in 1933. " The five senses play a primary role in the life of a child," he said, "and after sight, the sense of smell is, of course, predominant. If I wish to be transported to the past, nothing makes me experience it more vividly than recalling a particular scent." He wrote about a typical afternoon when "someone said the morels had appeared."

....the horses are put to the wagonette and we all drive to the woods. The ground is still soft and in places the wheels sink deep into the earth. We cannot drive up to the edge of the forest; there is still snow on the ground. We jump down and race into the woods. There is a smell of rotting leaves. We hallo to one another. Someone has found a morel and calls to the others. We cluster together, burrow among the leaves, clamber over a huge tree stump covered with dry twigs, over snail-clover and wood violets, paying no attention to them now, oblivious to everything but those little morels that have sprung up on their long legs. They seem to be hiding from us, covering themselves with leaves and moss, burying themselves under the brushwood; and what joy, what triumph, when at last we find one and put it in the basket. It smells like the leaves, like the forest, and like my blackened fingers...

Relatives, friends, scholars, and artists who visited the Tolstoys were treated to daytime activities from mushroom gathering and berry picking to tennis and swimming. Every evening family and guests engaged in conversation on almost every conceivable topic—literature, Russian politics, art, theories of education, music, religion, world history. Tokutomy Roka, a Japanese writer making a pilgrimage to visit Tolstoy, wrote a short essay about his experience on July 3, 1906, and titled it "Events of One Day."

It's my fourth day living in this house. I like the life here. Here is one of the summer days in Yasnaya Polyana.

Despite the early summer sunrise in Russia, the Tolstoy household sleeps until seven o'clock. The children rise earliest, and walk daily to the Zaseka station to pick up mail. The table under the maple is spread with a samovar, teacups, a cream pitcher, bread and plates, covered with a napkin to keep off the flies.

All come and go at will during breakfast. Tolstoy and the Countess rarely take breakfast. Tolstoy is usually busy with important affairs until noon.

Lunch is at twelve o'clock. A small bell hangs from the limb of an enormous elm. Family members gather from all parts as soon as the bell is rung. Lev

BATHHOUSE AT THE MIDDLE POND, YASNAYA POLYANA, 1905

Nikolaeyevich does not always come, but the hostess must. The men shake hands; the women kiss. Even during lunch, no one serves at table, and all feel quite free.

The time after lunch is for ambling, for riding a horse or a bicycle, or for swimming; some go strolling accompanied by the dogs.

Tolstoy is tormented by the insomnia of old age; he awakens five or six times nightly. Therefore he usually naps for an hour upon returning from his walk after lunch. As old Prince Bolkonsky (from War and Peace) used to say, a nap before dinner is precious.

The dinner bell rings at five or six o'clock. The whole family gathers round the table. Servants wait at table in tail-coats. A light appetizer is usually served. Lev Nikolayevich and the other men are dressed simply; the ladies do not change for dinner either.

Some walk after dinner, and others play tennis.

As soon as lights come on, the bell sounds evening tea.

They usually gather on the verandah. Tea, sweets, cherries, and raspberries are served. The women arrive with needlework; the men with books. All converse freely. These teatime conversations can last up to ten hours, and sometimes longer. This is how time is spent, whether with or without guests. Those who arrive are always received, and those who wish to leave are not detained. This life resembles the flow of water, or the whistling of the wind. There is a certain ease, cordiality, and sincerity all about. The attitude toward guests, toward servants, toward the people of the countryside, toward one another is natural, guileless, free, gracious, and sincere.

You can see how simply we live—the Countess said.

It is an enviable way to live—I answered.

There is, however, one "but"—Maria interjected

There are no "buts," I exclaimed, I envy the simple and natural life.

SONYA WITH DAUGHTERS MARIA, SASHA, AND FRIENDS AT THE BATHHOUSE ON THE VORONKA RIVER, YASNAYA POLYANA, 1896

DOMESTIC SCENE: SONYA WITH SON ANDREI AND DAUGHTER-IN-LAW SOPHIA IN THE MOSCOW HOUSE, KHAMOVNIKI, NOVEMBER 1895

ITALIAN LESSON: SONYA'S DAUGHTERS TANYA (FOREGROUND) AND MARIA (STANDING) WITH SERGEI TANEYEV, YASNAYA POLYANA, 1895

JULIA MARGARET CAMERON: "MADONNA WITH CHILDREN," CIRCA 1866, MUSEUM OF MODERN ART, NEW YORK

LADY CLEMENTINA HAWARDEN: "ISABELLA GRACE & FLORENCE ELIZABETH ON THE BALCONY OF 5 PRINCES GARDENS," CIRCA 1882, VICTORIA AND ALBERT MUSEUM, LONDON

LADY CLEMENTINA HAWARDEN: "[DAUGHTER] CLEMENTINA IN UNDERCLOTHES," 1860S, VICTORIA AND ALBERT MUSEUM, LONDON

Other Photographers

Affluent Women

SONYA WAS FAR FROM THE FIRST socially privileged woman to take up photography as a serious pastime. Amateurs famous in the two decades before Sonya photographed include Julia Margaret Cameron and Lady Clementina Hawarden.

Lady Hawarden, like Sonya, portrayed family and friends, and also like Sonya she posed them in domestic settings. One of Hawarden's 1860s pictures, "Clementina in Underclothes," brings to mind two of Sonya's self-portraits—the untitled 1897 photograph where Sonya stands in a posture reminiscent of Hawarden's girl near a picture of her deceased son Vanechka (p. 53); And "With Hyacinths in Moscow," featuring Sonya's profile, like Hawarden's daughter's, reflected dreamily in glass (p. 38).

Sonya's portraits and scenes are occasionally as elaborately styled as Hawarden's, but usually they are simpler, slightly more helter-skelter, and they are always more personal and convey an authenticity of emotion absent in the Englishwoman's work. Hawarden's 1862 "Isabella Grace & Florence Elizabeth," appears to depict a casual moment where one of the women, in the midst of a sisterly

GERTRUDE KÄSEBIER: "THE PICTURE BOOK," 1903, LIBRARY OF CONGRESS

embrace, glances away from the other toward the photographer. The photograph is beautiful. The women, devoid of emotion, are perfectly frozen in their pose. Compare this with Sonya's less perfect, more disorganized Italian lesson (p. 143), or her domestic sewing scene (p. 142), both made in 1895.

Julia Margaret Cameron was a prosperous Englishwoman married to a successful civil servant. Like Sonya, her roots were in the upper class. Unlike her she was after beauty rather than truth, though she meant to take reality into account. She made romantically lit portraits of famous acquaintances and staged poetic allegories using her friends, their relatives, and their servants as actors. Her portraits of literary and scientific men, including Tennyson, Longfellow, and Darwin, were haunting or mysterious. She was considered an amateur in her day, as was Sonya. Her standing as an artist came much later.

American photographer Gertrude Käsebier, photographing the same time as Sonya but very differently, had in common with both their predecessors the desire to create art. Käsebier devised sentimental fictions under the influence of Pictorialism, a photographic movement that had the lofty ambition of emulating classical painting. Sonya couldn't help being influenced by the painterly beauty to which the Pictorialists aspired, but she remained rooted in her journalistic mission.

Sonya composed her pictures formally, but within her compositions her subjects posed themselves spontaneously. By the real-life situations she selected and the fine-tuning of her framing, she could infuse her documentary approach with a touch of romance.

GERTRUDE KÄSEBIER: "THE WAR WIDOW," 1913, THE MUSEUM OF MODERN ART, NEW YORK

THE COOK, NIKOLAI MIKHAILOVICH RUMIANTSEV, AND THE NURSE FOR THE OLDER CHILDREN, MARIA AFANASIEVNA ARBUZOVA, YASNAYA POLYANA, 1897

Servants & Peasants

"...We took a long rest in the hut of some peasants who were working in the forest; they had a bonfire blazing, and those dark, ancient, majestic oaks soon made me forget my tiredness and I went home feeling happy and energetic." **23 August 1897**

"Complete chaos at home. The footman has fallen in love with Sasha the dressmaker and is going to marry her; Verochka, a mere baby of eighteen, is going to marry the bailiff on the 18th; the chef is leaving, and the cook has been taken off to hospital; Ilya and Nurse are in Moscow." **12 September 1898**

HOUSEHOLD SERVANTS AT YASNAYA POLYANA, 1895

TWO HUNDRED SERFS CAME with the land Tolstoy inherited in 1847. Their welfare was of concern to him almost immediately. He was attracted to them physically and drawn to them in principle. He saw peasant life as more wholesome than his own and closer to God, a useful model just when he was struggling to break his habits of gambling and whoring. He also recognized the horrifying injustice of a situation in which his life of privilege was made possible by the poverty of others.

Before marrying Tolstoy, Sonya didn't think much about the peasants' plight one way or the other. She accepted the status quo. She had a humane, even loving relationship with her servants, but she took them for granted. During the course of her marriage Sonya considered her husband's politics, confronted her feelings on the matter, and grew more sensitive to social injustice. Like others at the time she supported humanitarian causes. But she never understood Tolstoy's emotional relationship with the peasants, and she resented his willingness to give up the couple's way of life.

Aristocrats who mingled with the Russian peasantry in Tolstoy's day posed a serious threat to the social and political order. Government officials were alert to the precariousness of their positions in the face of such troublemakers: On December 14, 1825, a group of noblemen had staged an uprising in which they intended to obliterate existing class structure. Operating on behalf of all peasants, the leaders of the uprising aimed to right the wrongs inflicted on loyal peasant soldiers who fought against Napoleon's armies in 1812. This attempt at revolution failed, but the noblemen, known as the Decembrists, gained legendary status and provided inspiration for future generations.

Despite the Decembrists, Russian peasants before the middle of the 19th century were generally viewed by their owners as little more than animals. But at mid-century, change was in the air. Social unrest was growing. New literary works reflected the new mood: In his *Sketches From a Hunter's Album*, published in 1852, writer Ivan Turgenev presented the peasant as a human being with a capacity for practical work, rational thought, and noble ideals. The great Dostoevsky looked to the peasants for a key to the Russian soul and a path to Christ—but he astutely pointed out that though privileged Russians were drawn to folk culture, none of them really understood the peasants. The humble peasant—moral, simple, and pure—was, for the intelligentsia, merely theory.

In 1861 the Tsar issued a decree emancipating the serfs. The peasants became Russian citizens and were entitled to property. Tolstoy was appointed a magistrate in the Tula region where his estate was located to implement the Tsar's edict. He was probably the most open-handed property owner in Russia, giving generous portions of his own land to local peasants. He was always on the side of peasants making claims, and this made him unpopular with most of his fellow noblemen.

On March 1, 1881, revolutionaries assassinated the liberal Tsar Alexander II. In the immediate aftermath the government declared a state of emergency. The new, reactionary Tsar Alexander III clamped down with a repressive regime. There was a wave of pogroms, oppressive edicts against the Jews, new censorship laws, and the establishment of a political police force, the Okhrana. Tolstoy's devotion to the peasants remained unshaken, and he was popular enough to withstand mounting threats against him. The government calculated that arresting Tolstoy would result in mass resistance by unruly mobs.

While still a bachelor, Tolstoy fell in love with a peasant woman named Aksinia. She bore him a son before he married Sonya, and he continued to love her afterward. His attraction to her may have been based on her earthiness or her mystery; he clearly realized he didn't understand the shadings of the peasant mind or the subtleties of their society. In his great early novels he depicted the aristocracy with unsurpassed nuance whereas he expressed his feeling for the peasants indirectly. In *War and Peace* he described aristocratic Natasha's unforgettable, spontaneous dance in a forest cabin: As she abandoned herself to the dance, the culture of the Russian peasant, which was at the core of her being, rose up and revealed itself for the first time.

Throughout his life Tolstoy was burdened by internal contradictions and an agonized conscience. He found aristocratic life empty and meaningless, but could not walk away from that life. He labored in the fields with his peasants and afterward returned to dine with his family at a table served by white-gloved waiters. He tried endlessly to resolve these conflicts. He established peasant schools, made his own shoes, gave up the writing of novels, and preached his ideals of love to the peasants, welcoming his humble followers into his home to mingle with his refined family and elite guests. Sonya hated his followers and referred to them as "the dark ones."

In the 1890s Albert Shkarvan, a doctor, writer, and translator of Tolstoy's works into Slovak and German, was a guest at the Tolstoy house. In August 1896, he noted:

Tolstoy's followers dislike her, which is mutual, but to me personally she was sympathetic from beginning to end, and I respected her. As a mere mortal, I sympathized deeply with her, even in her starkly negative attitude toward "friends" of Tolstoy. She considered them to be benighted and unworthy hangers-on of her bright genius Lyova.

Though Sonya didn't agree with Tolstoy's approach to solving Russia's problems, she understood the magnitude of those problems. As always, she recorded her observations and opinions in her diary:

DIARY ENTRY **13 June 1902**

...He never stops working and is still writing his proclamation to the workers. I copied the whole thing out for him today. Much of it is illogical, impractical, and unclear. Either it will be very bad or he will have to do a lot more work on it. The fact that the land is owned by the rich, and the great suffering this imposes on the peasants, is indeed a crying injustice. But this matter will not be resolved in a hurry.

DIGGERS IN THE GARDEN AT THE LOWER POND, YASNAYA POLYANA, 1905

APPLE ORCHARD, YASNAYA POLYANA, AUTUMN 1897

APPLE HARVEST, YASNAYA POLYANA, 1897

PEASANTS AT WORK ON THE THRESHING GROUND, YASNAYA POLYANA, 1899

AS TIME WENT ON, TOLSTOY gained a larger and larger following for his social causes, and Sonya felt ever more trapped and angry. She lashed out at her husband and children and vented her emotions in her unflattering descriptions of people who showed up at the house.

DIARY ENTRY **17 December 1890**

...Some 'dark ones' have arrived: silly Popov, some weak, lazy Oriental, and stupid fat Khokhlov, who is of merchant origin. To think that these people are the great man's disciples—these wretched specimens of human society, windbags with nothing to do, wastrels with no education...

This did not endear her to her family. But like Tolstoy she was torn with conflict and she was complicated. In the summer of 1887, large numbers of needy peasants, many of them sick, appeared at Yasnaya Polyana daily. Sonya obtained a book of home remedies.

DIARY ENTRY **18 June 1887**

...Hordes of sick people visit me every day. I try, with the help of Floinskii's book, to treat them all, but what torture it is when I cannot recognize what is wrong and don't know what to do! It happens so often that I sometimes feel like abandoning the whole business, but then I go out and the sight of their sick pleading eyes and their touching trust makes me so sorry for them that although I dread to think I may be doing the wrong thing, I hand the poor dears their medicine and then try to put them right out of my mind. The other day I did not have the medicine I needed and had to give the poor woman a note and some money to take to the chemist. She burst into tears, returned the money and said: 'I know I am dying, so take back your money and give it to some worse off than me.'

VIEW OF MEADOW, FOREST, AND SMALL VORONKA RIVER IN THE ENVIRONS OF YASNAYA POLYANA, 1896

AT THE END OF 1890, several peasants, one by the name of Ilya Bolkhin, cut down 30 birch trees on the Tolstoy estate. At Sonya's instigation the peasants were legally charged with the offense. They were found guilty. The incident appears in the diaries of both Sonya and Lev.

DIARY ENTRY (SONYA) **11 December 1890**
...At the dinner-table Lyovochka told me that the peasants who'd been arrested for felling 30 trees in our birch wood were waiting outside to see me. Whenever I am told that someone is waiting to see me, and that I have to take some decision, I am seized with terror, I want to cry. Being expected to manage the estate and the house 'in a Christian spirit' is like being gripped in a vice, with no possible escape; it is a heavy cross to bear...

DIARY ENTRY (SONYA) **13 December 1890**
I did not write my diary yesterday—I was too distressed all day by thoughts of the peasants who were found guilty, although I did not know this until the evening....Today I learnt that the peasants had been sentenced to 6 weeks in jail and a 27-ruble fine. Once again a sob rose in my throat, and I have felt like weeping all day. I am sorry mainly for myself: why should people be harmed in my name, when I have nothing against them and would never wish anyone any harm? Even from a practical point of view, it is not my property, yet I have become a sort of scourge!

DIARY ENTRY (LEV) **15 December 1890**
Went out this morning and was met by Ilya Bolkhin begging for forgiveness: They've been sentenced to six weeks in jail. I was very depressed and my heart ached all day. Prayed, and will pray and go on praying....I must go away.

DIARY ENTRY (SONYA) **15 December 1890**
All of us here feel weighed down by a great melancholy. Lyovochka is even more sullen and out of sorts now that the peasants have been sentenced to hard labor for felling the trees in the plantation. Yet the moment it happened, immediately after the village policeman called, I asked him what I should do and whether they should be charged, and he pondered awhile then said: 'They should be given a good fright and then forgiven.' It soon turned out that this was a criminal offense, and that there was no chance of a pardon—so once again it was all my fault, of course. He is furious and won't speak, and I can't imagine what he is planning to do. I feel depressed, I'm sick and tired of the whole thing—I've had it up to my ears, as they say.

The Tolstoys' oldest son, Sergei, later said it was unlikely Tolstoy would have said the peasants, "should be given a fright." It would have been completely out of character. Sonya's diary and her memory were sometimes exaggerated in support of her viewpoint.

DIARY ENTRY (LEV) **16 December 1890**
Yesterday I went to bed and couldn't sleep. My heart ached, and above all I felt loathsome self-pity, and anger against her. An astonishing condition....Got out of bed at 2:00 and went into the drawing-room to walk about. She came out and we talked until after 4:00. The same as usual....I think I must declare to the government that I don't recognize property and royalties, and let them do as they will.

DIARY ENTRY (SONYA) **16 January 1891**
....I have decided to send Masha to help the families of those peasants who are in jail for stealing the wood.

Other Photographers

Social Documentary

MAXIM DMITRIEV: KRJUCHNIK THE PORTER, CARRIER OF WEIGHTS AND CARGO, RUSSIA, 1890S

PHOTOGRAPHY BY OUTSIDERS entered Tolstoy's household simply as a result of his great fame, and also because of specific projects he undertook on behalf of the peasants. One enterprise that brought photography to his attention came out of a national misfortune that upset him profoundly: In the early 1890s a sequence of crop failures gripped central Russia, and its aftermath, famine and disease, spread across the parched countryside. Tolstoy organized soup kitchens to alleviate the enormous suffering. He and his entire family, including Sonya and many volunteers, worked to distribute food and blankets.

While Tolstoy was organizing his relief program in 1891 and 1892 a photographer by the name of Maxim Petrovich Dmitriev, from the hard-hit region of Nizhny Novgorod, made forays into places most affected by the famine to photograph the starvation and consequent epidemics of cholera and typhus. In 1893 he produced an album of his work, "Crop Failure in the Nizhny Novgorod Province; photographed from life by M. Dmitriev." The stage-managed photographs, censored at the time, showed heart-wrenching scenes and were an unprecedented documentary accomplishment.

Dmitriev, knowing about Tolstoy's relief work, sent him a copy of his album and inscribed it, "To the great light in art and free thought, Count Lev Nikolaevich Tolstoy, from M. Dmitriev." Upon receiving the gift Tolstoy made a note to himself,

SOPHIA TOLSTOY: TATARS, KOREIZ, CRIMEA, 1901

SERGEY LOBOVIKOV: PEASANT SCENE, CIRCA 1909/10

"Author to be thanked." Dmitriev has since taken his place in photographic history as one of the first to successfully put the camera to use for a humanitarian cause. But even after seeing Dmitriev's work, Tolstoy never seriously considered the possibilities of photography as a tool for social change. This may be because photographs couldn't be easily disseminated at the time. Or it may simply be a failure of imagination—a rare thing for Lev Tolstoy.

Sonya, a social activist only when it came to supporting her husband—and rarely even then—had the sophisticated taste to appreciate Dmitriev's documentary accomplishment. She saw the world through refined eyes, was smart and enterprising, and kept up with developments

MAXIM DMITRIEV: TYPHUS VICTIM DURING FAMINE, KNJAGININE, NIZHNIY NOVGOROD, 1891/2

in photography. A major development that emerged worldwide in 1889 was Pictorialism, dedicated to elevating photography to an art.

Russian Pictorialism began in St. Petersburg and Moscow, then spread to the provincial intelligentsia. Some Pictorialists fabricated moody, soft-focus, fictional scenes, leaving everyday life behind altogether. Others produced painterly, Impressionist-style landscapes that were loosely rooted in the real world.

A few Russian Pictorialists—for example Nikolai Petrov, who was artistic director of the Pictorialist journal *Herald of Photography* (*Vestnik Fotografi*)—had international reputations. And one talent rose above the others: Sergei Lobovikov created noble, affectionate, sometimes dreamy images of peasant life as he saw it in his native town of Vyatka, just west of the Urals. But Lobovikov didn't turn away from the toughness of the peasants' circumstances: women in tattered clothes with their children, barefoot and grimy; peasants bent under heavy loads, working in their fields; families around humbly set tables; and the old tending the sick. His pictures showed a long-suffering population with enormous humanity and beauty. His fame spread outside Russia, and his photographs were exhibited in France and Germany. Lobovikov's portrayal of a noble peasantry coincided with Lev Tolstoy's political and romantic notions.

Sonya's natural and un-self-conscious humanism would have drawn her to this work. Her photography of peasants was far less accomplished than Lobovikov's. In the few pictures she took on this subject she kept to her own unwavering and focused documentary purpose and style.

SERGEI LOBOVIKOV: PEASANT SCENE, CIRCA 1907-10

THE KOSLOVA-ABATIS RAILWAY STATION, SUMMER 1897

THE SUMMER SONYA TOOK this picture, Tolstoy was proposed as a candidate for the Nobel Peace Prize and was working on his book What is Art? Industrialization was changing the face of Russia, town life was overtaking rural, the railroads were expanding.

Sonya's son Andrei had taken up photography, and she was pleased. He participated in the making of this railway station picture, a fact Sonya noted in her photographic records with the words "taken by me and Andryusha." but this son's irresponsibility was a source of constant aggravation and occasional anguish.

DIARY ENTRY **23 July 1897**
Andryusha has squandered all his money on the gypsies again, and has borrowed 300 rubles. I am depressed and disgusted by his appalling life. What will become of him? He has already gone to the bad, and the worst of it all is that he has taken to drink, and he's a complete dare-devil when he is drunk.

But as always, Sonya found time for her poetic musings and for photography.

DIARY ENTRY **18 August 1897**
...I took a lovely walk through Zaseka, then along the railway tracks to Kozlovka....In the forest I was in a state of poetic peace such as I have not felt for a long time. But then I overtired myself; we covered about 12 versts (1.1 km, about .66 mi.) and it became dull and hard going...

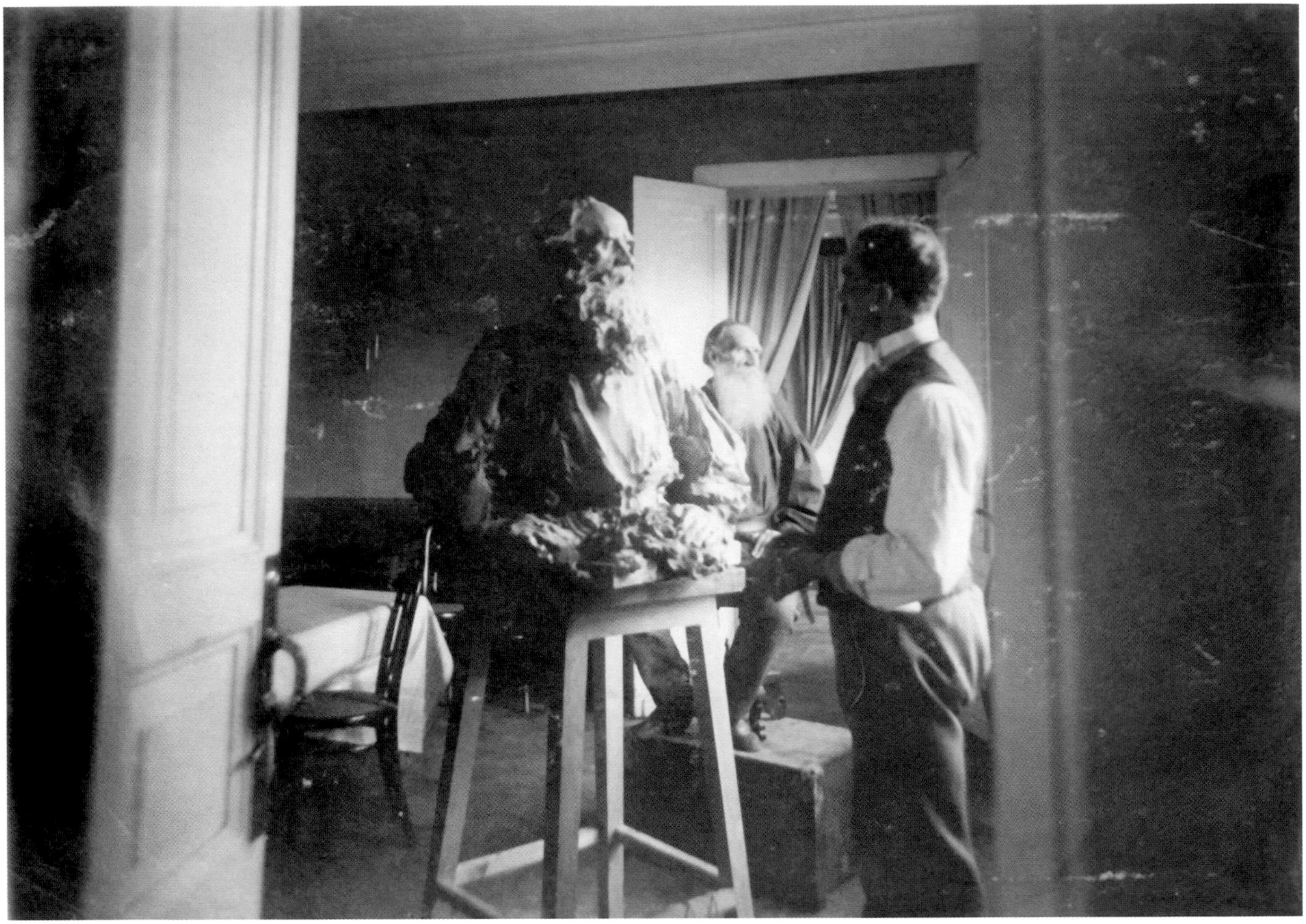

TOLSTOY SITTING FOR SCULPTOR PAVEL TRUBETSKOI IN THE DINING ROOM OF THE MOSCOW HOUSE, APRIL 1898

Artists

"What is so interesting about Lev Nikolaevich's life? Or Sergei Ivanovich's? We love them not for their lives, or how they appear to us, but for that dream, deep and endless, from which their art flows; it is this we love to sense and idealize in them.

23 October 1897

LEV TOLSTOY POSING FOR SCULPTOR ILYA YAKOVLEVICH GINSBURG, YASNAYA POLYANA, 1897 (BOTH)

LEV TOLSTOY POSING FOR SCULPTOR ILYA YAKOVLEVICH GINSBURG, YASNAYA POLYANA, 1897

SCULPTURE BY I. Y. GINSBURG

A PARADE OF PAINTERS AND SCULPTORS made the pilgrimage to Yasnaya Polyana to depict Tolstoy for posterity. Ilya Yakovlevich Ginsburg was one of those who often visited and worked at the Tolstoy estate. Ginsburg was an accomplished sculptor. He was admitted to the St. Petersburg Academy of Arts in 1878 and received a gold medal in 1886 for his bas-relief titled "Lamentations of Prophet Jeremiah on the Ruins of Jerusalem." His long career took him well into the Soviet era. His specialty was portrait statuettes of artistic and cultural luminaries. This one of Tolstoy is only about 12 inches tall.

Tolstoy couldn't bear to sit for long periods and he complained that he was uncomfortable with the idea of his personal fame. Sonya's photographs helped take the pressure off and were useful to the artists. They sometimes asked her to photograph specific poses. The influence her work had upon some of their productions is obvious.

LEV TOLSTOY AND ANTON CHEKHOV IN GASPRA, CRIMEA, SEPTEMBER 1901

TOLSTOY AND THE WRITER Anton Chekhov liked each other. Chekhov first visited Tolstoy at his estate in August 1895. The two men stayed in touch, and when Tolstoy was in the Crimean town of Gaspra recuperating from an illness, Chekhov visited him there, and Sonya made a photograph to mark the occasion.

Chekhov had been attracted to Tolstoy's blend of beliefs (referred to as Tolstoyism) a decade before the two men met. He may have been sympathetic to Tolstoy's anti-materialism in part because he grew up in a poor family and his grandfather had been a serf, but after six years under the spell of its persuasive idealism he walked away from its extreme principles. Swinging from devotion to opposition, he repudiated Tolstoy's views about the peasants and the government as not only illogical and unjust but also arrogant, stubborn, and ignorant. However he still revered Tolstoy's literary genius.

When they finally met, Chekhov was hypnotized by Tolstoy's powerful personality, and Tolstoy was captivated by Chekhov's charm. Sonya was also drawn to Chekhov. She even hoped, briefly, that the 35-year-old writer would be attracted to her 31-year-old daughter Tanya. That didn't happen, but Chekhov was impressed with the Tolstoy girls. In a letter to his friend Alexei Suvorin, editor of the newspaper *New Times*, he wrote, *Tolstoy's daughters are very attractive. They worship their father and cherish a fanatic belief in him. And that means that Tolstoy is indeed a great moral force, for if he were insincere and not above reproach the first to be skeptical of him would be his daughters, because daughters are like sparrows: they are not to be caught with chaff....You can fool your fiancée or your mistress to the top of your bent, and in the eyes of his beloved even an ass appears to be a philosopher, but daughters are a different kettle of fish.*

Sonya enjoyed Chekhov's literary work and she loved their conversations, particularly about the publishing enterprise she was engaged in at the time. It had been no small effort to get her venture going. Her plan had evolved after years of worrying about the depletion of the family finances. She had also wanted to find an additional way to serve her husband's writing talent. A publishing business to sell Tolstoy's work seemed like the perfect thing. In the process of thinking it over, Sonya had been encouraged by the business accumen of Fyodor Dostoevsky's widow, Anna Grigoryevna, who printed and distributed Dosteovsky's work after he died in 1881. Sonya had appealed to Anna for advice, and the two became friends.

Tolstoy thought this focus on money was trivial, felt his work should be public property, and was appalled by Sonya's idea. They argued, but in 1885 she established a publishing office and warehouse in a shed on their Moscow property. Sonya's energy and practical nature led to a respectable though modest degree of business success.

As Tolstoy's fame grew, Russian artists, writers, and scholars increasingly made pilgrimages to the Tolstoy estate. Many came from abroad, some from great distances, to be in the legendary man's presence and hear his sometimes brilliant, sometimes troubling ideas. But writer Ivan Turgenev lived only about 50 miles from Yasnaya Polyana and didn't need to go out of his way to spend time with his neighbor. The two writers knew each other from youth.

Over the years Tolstoy and Turgenev had their differences and occasional quarrels—Tolstoy was abrasive; Turgenev thought the first two sections of *War and Peace* were tedious and he challenged Tolstoy's negative portrayal of women. They made amends more than once, but the chemistry between them wasn't quite right and they never had a close or easy friendship. Nevertheless, they held each other in high regard and now and then sought each other out.

In 1883, on his deathbed in Bougival, near Paris, Turgenev wrote Tolstoy one final letter:

June 28, 1883

Dear and cherished Lev Nikolayevich!

I have not written to you for a long time for I have been and am, to speak frankly, in a dying state....I write you, really, to tell you how happy I am to have been your contemporary, and to express to you my last request. My friend, return to your literary activity. You have, you know, that gift from whence all other things come. Oh, how happy I should be if I could think that my request would have its effect!...My friend, great writer of our Russian land, do heed my request. Let me know if you receive this note and allow me to embrace you once more affectionately, and your wife, all of you...I cannot write any more....I am tired.

Turgenev died two months later, on August 22.

SONYA DIDN'T THINK MUCH OF most likenesses of her husband. She wrote in her unpublished autobiography My Life (*Moya Zhizn*), "...not one of the sculptures representing him has managed to convey his true appearance. The best one is the small bust with folded arms by Trubetskoi. "

In spring 1898 Pavel Trubetskoi came to Yasnaya Polyana and spent exactly two weeks working on the bust Sonya refers to. During the ordeal Ivan Gorbunov, a well-known actor, writer, and an old family friend, read aloud to Tolstoy, who was as restless as ever. Sonya photographed the scene and recorded her unfolding impressions in her diary:

DIARY ENTRY **15 April 1898**

This evening we had a visit from young Prince Trubetskoi, a sculptor born and educated in Italy. An extraordinary man, exceptionally talented, but utterly primitive. He hasn't read a thing, doesn't even know War and Peace, *hasn't studied anywhere—he is naïve, rough, and totally engrossed in his art. He is coming here tomorrow to start on a sculpture of Lev Nikolaevich, and he will dine with us.*

DIARY ENTRY **16 April 1898**

Lev Nikolaevich was sculpted today by Prince Trubetskoi, who has come from Italy and is in fact an Italian citizen. He is apparently considered a very good sculptor. Nothing visible so far. He has made a start on a huge bust.

DIARY ENTRY **18 April 1898**

Trubetskoi has done more work on his sculpture of Lev Nikolaevich, and I can now see how exceptionally talented he is.

DIARY ENTRY **19 April 1898**

Trubetskoi is still working on his bust of Lev Nikolaevich, and it's extremely good—majestic, distinctive and very lifelike. This Trubetskoi is a naïve fellow, completely absorbed in his art; he has read nothing and is interested in nothing but sculpture.

DIARY ENTRY **29 April 1898**

Trubetskoi finished his bust of Lev Nikolaevich on the 23rd and it is excellent.

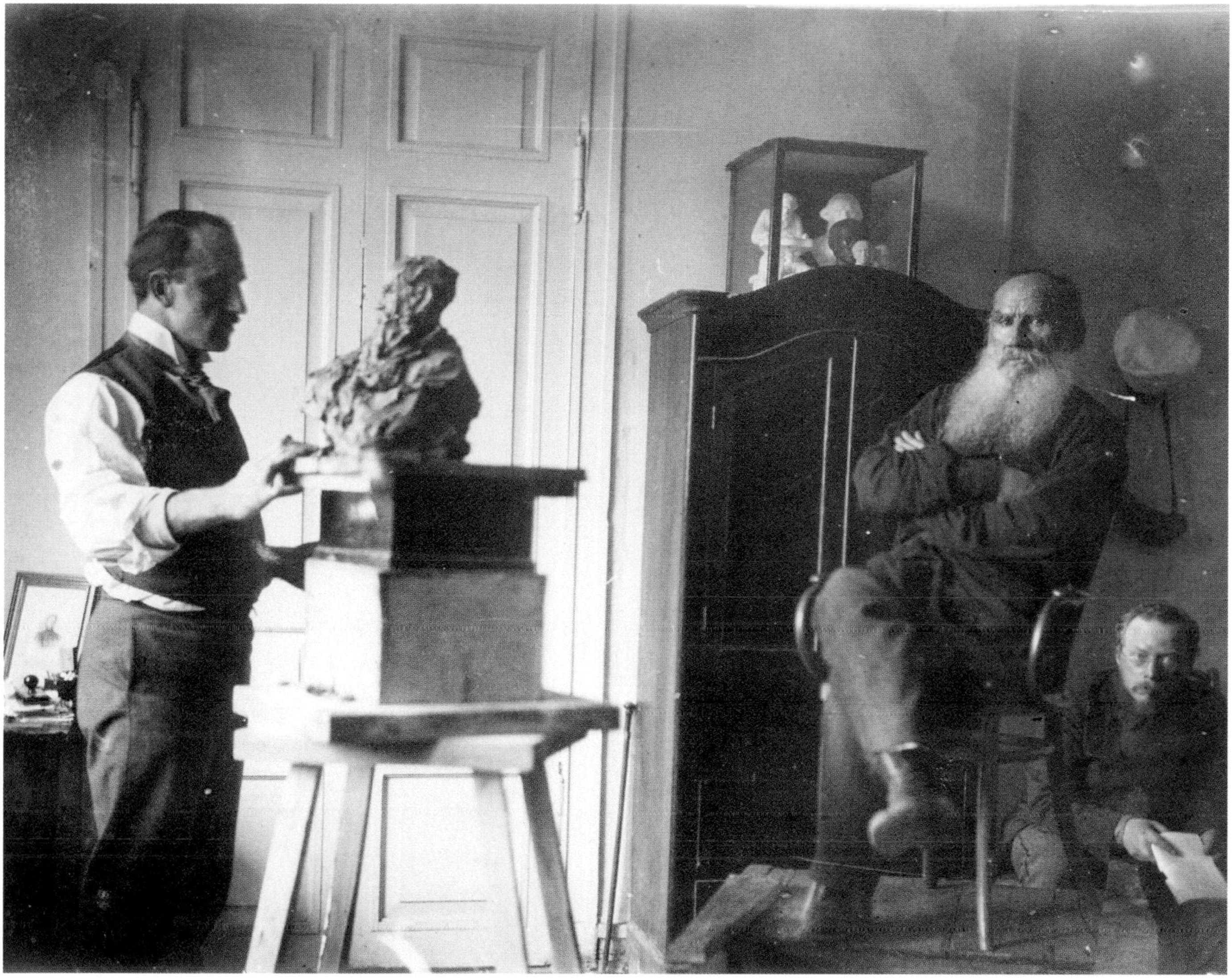

PAVEL TRUBETSKOI MODELS TOLSTOY'S BUST WHILE IVAN GORBUNOV READS ALOUD TO HIM, YASNAYA POLYANA, AUGUST 28, 1899 (TOLSTOY'S 71ST BIRTHDAY)

LEV AND SONYA TOLSTOY WITH ILYA GINSBURG (LEFT) AND VLADIMIR STASOV, YASNAYA POLYANA, AUGUST 9, 1900

IN 1870, 14 YOUNG ARTISTS turned away from classical European art and biblical themes, broke with Russia's official Academy of Arts, and formed the Fellowship of Wandering Artists. Their goal was twofold—to depict the common people with honesty and sensitivity and to bring their art to these same people in order to raise social awareness. Their mission was to find the ideal in contemporary Russian reality.

The Wanderers, or Itinerants as these artists were sometimes called, were not operating in a void. In the 1860s and 70s, traditional political and social institutions were being actively challenged by a broad range of well-meaning, upper-class liberals who wanted to extend education and health services to the peasantry. Radical students who advocated revolution were also active at the time.

In 1874, thousands of student revolutionaries calling themselves Populists streamed into the countryside with ideas of linking their lives to the peasants in brotherhood, socialism, and hard work. But the peasants they encountered were uncomprehending and suspicious, and in some cases even went so far as to report them to the authorities. Arrested or forced underground, the Populists had to admit defeat, temporarily at least. In contrast the Itinerants, who were not as directly political, took their work on the road successfully. They were welcomed in rural villages, their paintings were greeted with interest and conversation, and their exhibitions were special occasions.

Vladimir Stasov, a passionate critic and scholar, led the charge to liberate Russian art from Western Europe. He discovered and championed many of the artists who filled the ranks of the new nationalist movement, among them Ivan Kramskoi and Ilya Repin. He was a great admirer of Tolstoy and a frequent visitor to Yasnaya Polyana. The Tolstoys' youngest daughter, Sasha, recalled that Stasov often came to the house with sculptor Ilya Ginsburg. "It would be difficult to imagine two people more different in appearance than these two friends," she recalled.

Ginsburg, a modest man, was short swarthy, bald, with fiery black eyes, tiny hands, a thin voice. Stasov was a man of tremendous stature, of heroic proportions, with a long beard and a thick head of hair. When he spoke it was not with simple tones but with the utterance of a prophet, attracting the attention of all.

Sonya arranged a summer photograph in which she positioned Stasov between her husband and Ginsburg; then, outfitted in elegant finery, she joined the composition next to her peasant-frocked husband.

She recorded an earlier winter visit by the same guests.

DIARY ENTRY **3 January 1898**

Ginsburg the sculptor, a young painter, and Vereshchagin (a bad writer) were here yesterday morning. Stasov took advantage of his 74 years to fling his arms around me and kiss me, repeating 'Oh, how pink and how slender you are!' I was so embarrassed—I just couldn't get away from him. We then went upstairs to the drawing-room and discussed Lev Nikolaevich's article "On Art." Stasov said he thought L. N. had got it all back to front. He didn't have to tell me that, he certainly hit the nail on the head.

Sonya was exaggerating Stasov's position. In fact, he wrote in a letter dated January 9, 1898,

"I too am in indescribable ecstasy over that marvelous article "On Art," despite the fact that I do not agree with everything in it." But Sonya had become emotional about this topic and felt vindicated by every negative comment she heard. "On Art" had entered the realm of their larger quarrel.

DIARY ENTRY **13 August 1897**

I have copied out a great deal of Lev Nikolaevich's manuscript "On Art" recently. I spoke to him about it yesterday, and asked him how he expected art to exist without all the specialist 'schools' he attacks. But one can never have a discussion with him; he always gets dreadfully irritable and shouts, and it all becomes so unpleasant that one loses sight of the subject under discussion, and merely wants him to stop talking as soon as possible. And that's what happened yesterday.

When our guests were here he read them this article and no one said a word. They were right to let him think they agreed with it all. And it does contain some admirable ideas, such as that art should inspire, not merely entertain; this is unquestionably true. And that drawing, music, and all the arts should be taught in the schools, so that every individual with talent may discover his own path; another splendid idea.

DIARY ENTRY **3 January 1898**

There were noisy, heated discussions about art. Stasov said nothing, L. N. shouted, and Rimsky-Korsakov launched into a passionate defense of beauty in art, saying that people must be educated to appreciate it. All this is discussed in his article. None of us agreed with L. N.'s denial of beauty, and the level of development required to understand art.

Tolstoy was the perfect subject for the new socially conscious generation of painters and sculptors. In their portraiture they often were after more than mere physical likeness. They wanted portrayals of Russian virtue. Nikolai Gué, who had previously painted gospel subjects, was a case in point. He made Tolstoy's portrait in 1884 at the family's Moscow estate, Khamovniki. In addition to admiring Tolstoy's literary genius, Gué was a believer in his philosophy. He meant to express both concepts in his painting.

The first of the Itinerants to come to Yasnaya Polyana was Ivan Kramskoi, co-founder of the movement, prolific art critic, and master portraitist. Kramskoi arrived while Tolstoy was writing *Anna Karenina*. Sonya noted his visit in her diary.

DIARY ENTRY **4 October 1873**

Kramskoi is doing two portraits of L., and this tends to prevent him working. But to make up for it there are long discussions and arguments about art everyday.

After his visit to Yasnaya Polyana on February 23, 1874, Kramskoi wrote to the Itinerant painter Ilya Repin that Tolstoy, "is an interesting, even extraordinary man. I spent several days with him, and I confess I was in a state of agitation throughout. He smacks of genius." Ilya Repin subsequently became a Yasnaya Polyana regular.

LEV TOLSTOY POSING FOR SCULPTOR ILYA GINSBURG, YASNAYA POLYANA, 1900 (BOTH)

ILYA REPIN, YASNAYA POLYANA, SEPTEMBER 23, 1907

DIARY ENTRY **19 August 1887**

The painter Repin visited on the 9th and left on the night of the 16th. He did two portraits of Lev Nikolaevich; the first he started painting in the study downstairs, but he was not satisfied with it and started on another in the drawing room upstairs, against a bright background. It is extraordinarily good, and is still drying. The first he finished in a rough and ready fashion and gave to me.

The Tolstoys' daughter Tanya, who grew up to become an aspiring painter herself, wrote to her friend Elizaveta Olsufieva about the second portrait, the one that was still drying: "On the first day of his visit here Repin sketched Papa in various poses, in his album, in order to familiarize himself with him, and yesterday he started on his large portrait in oils. By today he had already finished the whole head and it is marvelous, in both the execution and the expression. He managed to capture that good sweet expression on Papa's face, which neither Gué or Kramskoi was able to convey."

Ilya Repin eventually painted more portraits of Tolstoy than any other artist. Whenever he was in Tolstoy's presence he, like his colleague Ivan Kramskoi, fell under Tolstoy's powerful spell. But when he'd leave, his mind would clear and he would find himself considering Tolstoy's dual lifestyle, questioning his philosophy, and doubting the authenticity of his relationship to the peasants.

Sonya in her diary entry of June 29, 1891, noted, "Repin is obviously jaded by life." But despite his doubts, Repin recognized Tolstoy's genius and was in awe of him. And Sonya, for her part, put aside the evaluation of Repin's outlook, and kept track of the painter's work.

LEV TOLSTOY AND ILYA REPIN IN THE PARLOR AT YASNAYA POLYANA, DECEMBER 17, 1908

DIARY ENTRY **16 July 1891**

....We had crowds of visitors here. Repin left today; he has finished a small head and shoulders of Lyovochka writing in his study, and has started a larger full-length painting of him standing barefoot in the forest with his hands in his belt. He is going to finish this one at home.

In September 1907, Sonya mimicked a Repin painting in a photograph she staged of herself with Tolstoy in his study. Two months later she began a painted copy of the same double portrait. She prepared a canvas, traced Repin's painting onto it, worked on it for several weeks, and photographed herself with the result (following pages).

LEV AND SONYA TOLSTOY IN TOLSTOY'S STUDY, YASNAYA POLYANA, SEPTEMBER 23, 1907
(SONYA'S NOTE FOR THIS PHOTOGRAPH READS: "L. N. AND ME IN THE ATTITUDE OF REPIN'S PORTRAIT.")

SONYA PAINTS A COPY OF THE PORTRAIT BY ILYA REPIN.

PAINTING SESSION: TANYA KUZMINSKAYA (SONYA'S SISTER) SITS FOR THREE WOMEN PAINTERS, INCLUDING TANYA TOLSTOY (SONYA'S DAUGHTER). OTHER RELATIVES LOOK ON, YASNAYA POLYANA, JULY 1898

Sonya was a religious woman. She prayed, observed the feast days, and placed her destiny in God's hands. Life would have been empty without the knowledge that she and her family were part of God's spiritual plan.

Though she wouldn't have said so, her relationship to art bore some resemblance to her relationship to religion. She looked to art for spiritual fulfillment and for meaning in perpetuity. But the similarity between art and religion had its limitations. Religion was based on faith, its tenets came down to believers from history and authority, and Sonya accepted that, whereas she was ready to question even the most popular art of the day, as she did when she visited the 26th exhibition of paintings by the Fellowship of Wandering Artists.

DIARY ENTRY **15 April 1898**

We had guests this evening, including professor Preobrazhenskii, who took our photographs with magnesium plate and read us a long lecture on illusions of light and color. I was worn out and grew sleepy, something that rarely happens to me. Earlier on I had taken Sasha to the traveling art show: there was nothing outstanding, apart from some good late landscapes by Shishkin, and the general poverty of subject matter and content was appalling.

In the case of art, Sonya's mind was demanding. She spent time with work she liked, probing and evaluating its layers of composition, color, and emotional content. Her diary entry of April 15 goes on to praise a less popular exhibition:

Yesterday I spent two and a half hours at an exhibition of St. Petersburg painters [the 6th exhibition of paintings by the St. Petersburg Society of Artists], *with an enormous painting by Semidarskii of a woman martyr tied to a bull in a circus, with Nero, etc. I was fascinated by this exhibition. There was a great variety of landscapes, taking me first to Italy, then to the Crimea, then to the River Dnieper, then to the island of Capri—to wild Oriental countries, or the Russian or Little Russian countryside, or the Caucasus. It was extremely interesting, especially for me, who have never traveled anywhere. Almost all the paintings were well and carefully executed—though not all of them showed evidence of talent. "Circe the Christian in Nero's Circus" was a huge painting occupying one large wall. People have expressed various guarded opinions about it, but I personally thought it very beautiful and vivid, and the characters, colors, and proportions very harmonious and intelligent. But it's cold; one doesn't pity the martyr torn to pieces, one doesn't pity the bull with the beautiful head, and one doesn't feel angry with Nero—one doesn't feel the public is affected by it. But the exhibition in general gave me immense pleasure.*

Sonya loved to encourage creativity in others, especially in her daughter Tanya, for whom she obtained instruction from the best Russian artists of the day, including Repin. And her lifelong desire to create her own art impelled her to throw herself boldly into various media, including painting, which she took up in 1900. Her watercolors of herbs on the Yasnaya property are not only lovely, they reveal the existence in Tolstoy's day of plant life that would otherwise remain unknown.

SONYA SITS FOR DAUGHTER TANYA AND SCULPTOR ILYA GINSBURG IN TANYA'S STUDIO, YASNAYA POLYANA, JULY/AUGUST 1897

HERB, YASNAYA POLYANA, N.D.

SONYA'S HERB PAINTINGS, YASNAYA POLYANA

LEV AND SONYA TOLSTOY, YASNAYA POLYANA, AUGUST 1, 1901

Illness

*"I am terrified not by the thought of death—
for I welcome that—but of a helpless old age!"*

13 July 1897

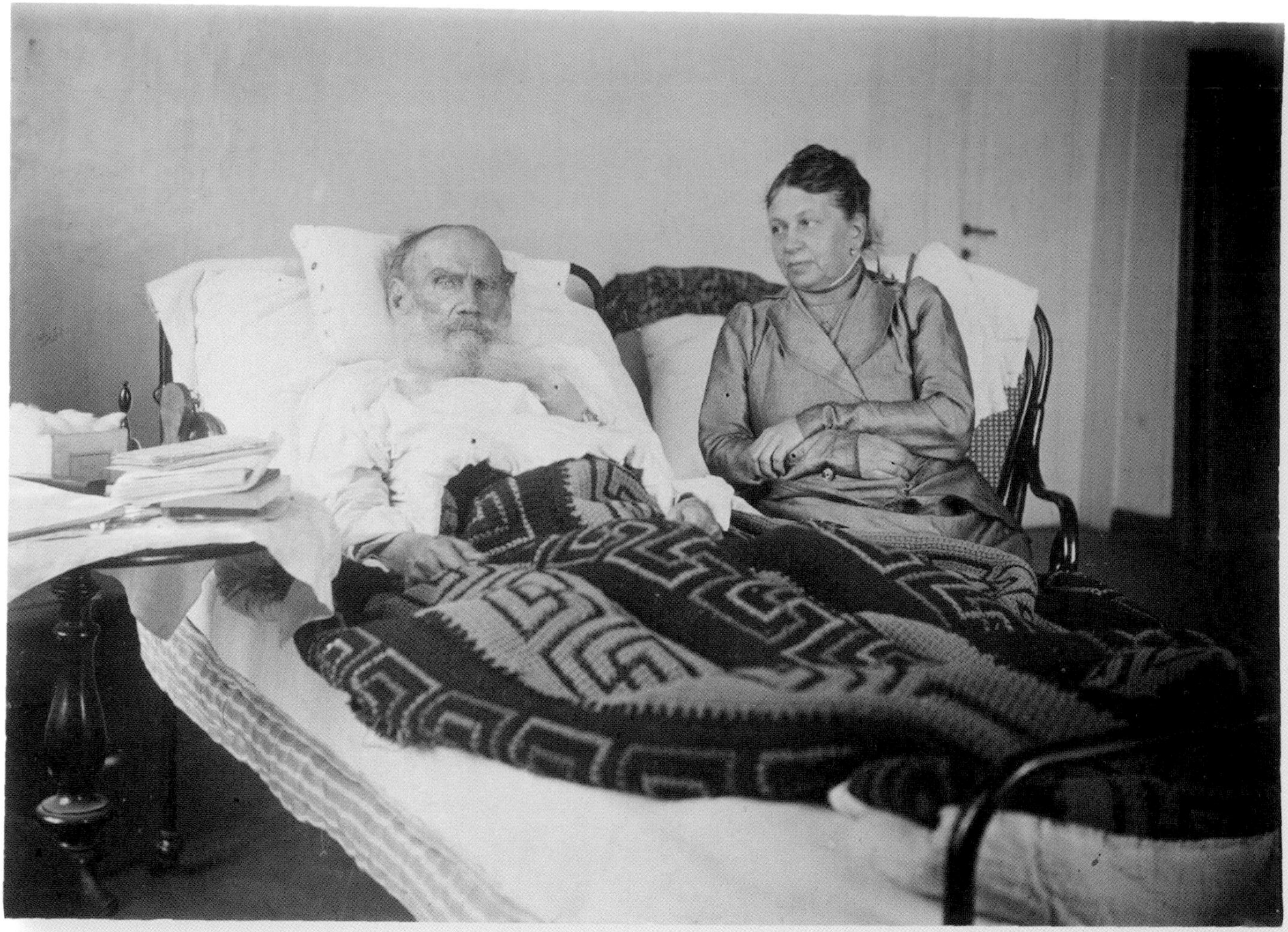

GASPRA, CRIMEA, MAY 1902

IN LATE JUNE 1901, TWO MONTHS before Tolstoy turned 73, he was diagnosed with malaria. It was a severe case and he had heart problems as well. As always when he was sick, Sonya nursed him and they drew close for a spell. Doctors were called, quinine was prescribed, and Tolstoy began to recover. But recovery was brief, and this illness seemed different from earlier episodes.

DIARY ENTRY (SONYA) **3 July 1901**

Something frightful is drawing near, and although everyone anticipates it yet it is utterly unexpected when it comes—it is death, and the death of someone whose life means far more to me than my own, because I have lived exclusively through Lyovochka and the children he has given me…Yesterday morning I was putting a hot compress on his stomach when he suddenly gazed intently at me and began to weep, saying: 'Thank you Sonya. You mustn't imagine that I am not grateful to you or that I don't love you…' And his voice broke with emotion and I kissed his dear familiar hands, telling him what pleasure it gave me to look after him, and how guilty I felt when I could not make him completely happy, and begging him to forgive me for being unable to do so. Then we both wept and embraced. For such a long time my soul has yearned for this—a deep and serious recognition of our closeness over the thirty-nine years we have lived together.

DIARY ENTRY (LEV) **16 July 1901**

Haven't written in my diary for more than a month. Was seriously ill from 27 June, and before that was unwell for a couple of weeks. My illness was one long spiritual holiday; heightened spirituality, and calmness at the approach of death, and expressions of love from all sides…

DIARY ENTRY (SONYA) **30 July 1901**

L. N. was poorly again yesterday evening. He had a bad attack of indigestion, an accumulation of bile and a fever: at 11 p.m. yesterday the thermometer showed a temperature of 37.8° and his pulse was around 90 all day….I lead a dreary life, sitting all day by my sick husband's door and knitting caps for the orphanage. All the life and energy in me has died. I received a letter from Countess Panina offering us her dacha, Gaspra, in the Crimea, and we are planning to go, although I don't want to leave before September.

DIARY ENTRY (LEV) **18 August 1901**

…During this time it's been decided we should go to the Crimea. I'm rather pleased about it. My health is much weaker: my heart is weaker. But I'm improving and, unfortunately, I've lost the élan I had during my illness.

On September 5 Lev and Sonya, accompanied by a small entourage of family and supporters, left Yasnaya Polyana for Tula by carriage and from there traveled southeast in a luxurious private train car. At every place they stopped, first at Kursk and then at Kharkov, and finally when the group disembarked at Sevastopol, throngs of admirers and well-wishers surged onto the station platforms to cheer Tolstoy and wish him well. Two carriages took the travelers on to the Black Sea coast and to Gaspra.

Gaspra, the manor house owned by the wealthy and gracious Countess Sophia Vladimirovna Panina, was luxurious in the extreme, an uncomfortable fact for Tolstoy, but the warm air was soothing, the view of the sea was pleasant, and in any case he had other things to think about.

THE TOLSTOYS STAYED IN GASPRA nearly a year. Despite Sonya's focus on her husband's health during that time, or maybe in part because of it, she photographed a great deal. A constant stream of family, friends, doctors, and other well-wishers made the pilgrimage to Gaspra, stayed some time, or passed through briefly. Sonya photographed them in groups or alone with Tolstoy, on the terrace, on the balcony, on estate grounds and by the sea. She photographed Tolstoy with and without herself in the frame and Tolstoy seems to have borne it all relatively patiently if not happily—or maybe he had little choice. The contrast between the intensity of his eyes and the frailty of his body suggests his mind was churning with life while he was physically getting weaker.

Artists and friends who saw Sonya's Crimean photographs admired them enormously. Her pictures were intimate and lively. Vladimir Stasov, the art and music critic, spoke especially highly of her work. Yet Sonya barely mentioned her photographic activity in her diary. Her mind was filled with the particulars of Tolstoy's health, and her outlook on life was determined by his attitude toward her at any given moment. His health and both their moods swung incessantly from high to low, and that is what she documented.

DIARY ENTRY **2 December 1901**

And as for the spiritual and physical solitude I experienced last night! Things have happened exactly as I imagined they would. Now that physical infirmity has forced Lev Nikolaevich to abandon amorous relations with his wife (this was not so long ago), instead of that peaceful affectionate friendship which I have longed for in vain all my life, there remains nothing but complete emptiness.

Morning and evening he greets me and leaves me with a cold and formal kiss. He calmly accepts my anxieties about him as his due, he frequently loses his temper and tends to regard the world about him with utter indifference, and there are now only two things that excite, interest, and torment him in the material and intellectual realms—death and his work.

Tolstoy's preoccupation with death long preceded the family's sojourn in Gaspra. His nearly lifelong concern with it was part intellectual, part spiritual, and certainly personal. He managed to consider his own death somewhat calmly as it got closer.

DIARY ENTRY (LEV) **3 January 1904**

Am I afraid of death? No. But at the approach of death or the thought of it, I can't help experiencing the sort of trepidation that a traveler must experience as he approaches the place where his train drops down to the sea from an enormous height, or who rises to an enormous height in a balloon. The traveler knows that nothing will happen to him, that it will only be the same as happens to millions of creatures, that he will only change his method of travel, but he can't help experiencing trepidation as he approaches the place. Such is my feeling too about death.

Sonya's relationship to death was concrete, emotional, and tied to specific individuals, especially Tolstoy and their children. Only rarely did she wonder about it abstractly, as she did passingly in a diary entry on March 1, 1898: "*What is death? We go off somewhere and fuse with eternity, guided by the same Will which guides us here on earth.*" But her belief in God and an afterlife never offered her any real consolation.

TOLSTOY IN WHEELCHAIR ON LOWER TERRACE AT GASPRA WITH SON SERGEI, DAUGHTER MASHA, SONYA, AND OTHERS, CRIMEA, APRIL 1902

TOLSTOY WITH HIS SISTER MARIA ON THE BALCONY AT THE GASPRA VILLA, CRIMEA, 1901/2

TOLSTOY WITH DR. L. B. BERTENSON, GASPRA, CRIMEA, JUNE 4, 1902

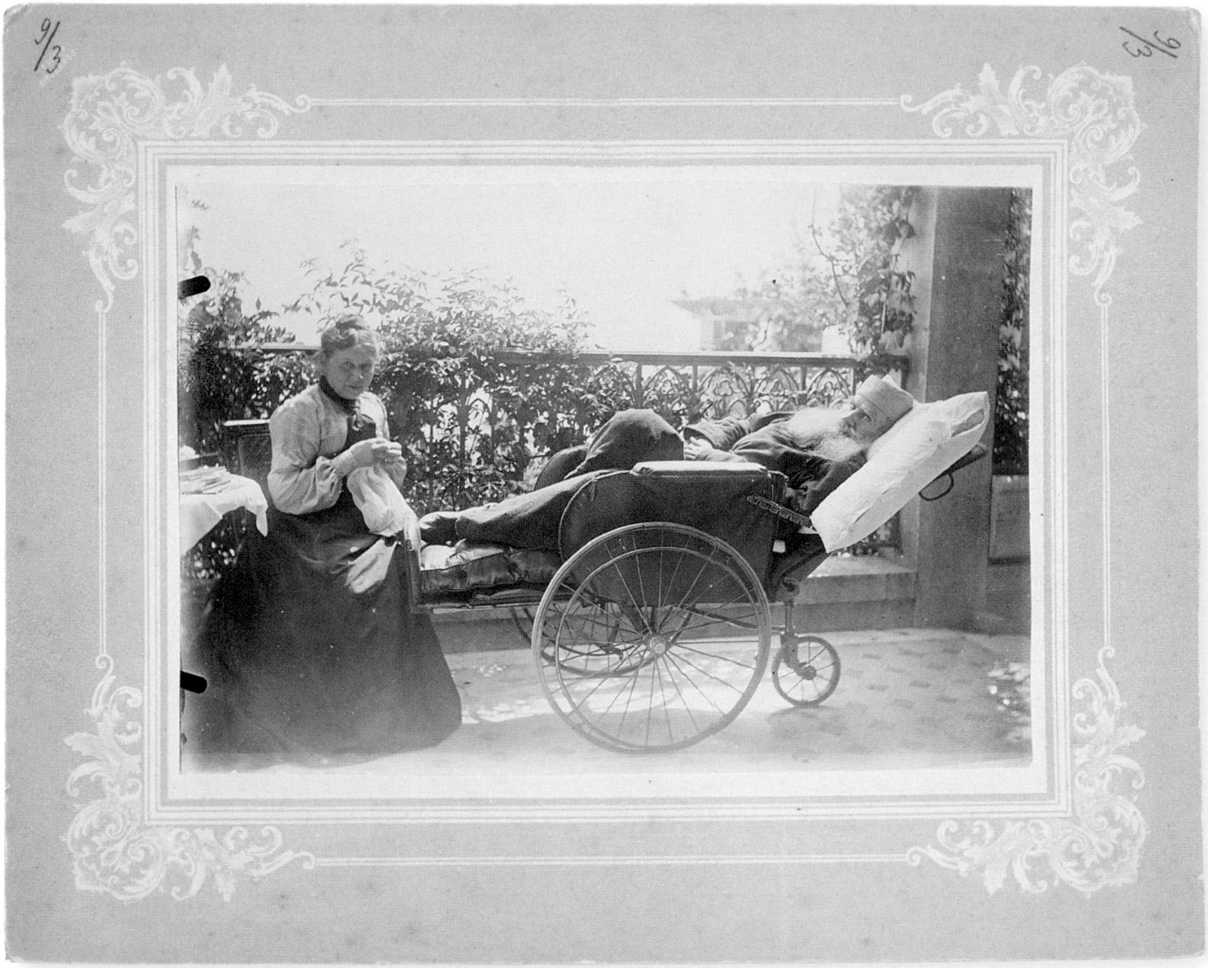

LEV AND SONYA TOLSTOY, GASPRA, CRIMEA, MAY 2, 1902

RELIGION WAS MUCH ON THE MINDS of the Tolstoys. Just six months before traveling to Gaspra, on February 24, 1901, Tolstoy had been formally excommunicated by the Orthodox Church as a result of his outspoken repudiation of its institutions and his ridicule of its ritual. Sonya, defending her husband as always, wrote a letter to the Holy Synod protesting the excommunication. She herself had faith in Orthodoxy, she wrote, nevertheless one doesn't have to be a member of the Church to be a good Christian, and as far as she was concerned her husband led a more Christian life than some ecclesiastics in the Church's upper echelons. The Holy Synod responded by affirming the excommunication.

In Gaspra a few months later, Tolstoy worked

on an article titled, "What is Religion and What is its Essential Nature?" In his diary he kept track of his progress.

DIARY ENTRY (LEV) **10 October 1901**

I've been working all this time on "Religion." I think it's progressing, but I've become mentally weaker; I can't work so long.

DIARY ENTRY (LEV) **November 1901**

I think I've finished "On Religion." As always, I doubt the importance and goodness of this work, but with more justification now, I think, than on previous occasions.

DIARY ENTRY (LEV) **26 December 1901**

I've finished On Religion. But I'll probably revise it again. I've been writing about religious tolerance for about ten days, and am bored with it. It's too unimportant.

In the meantime all kinds of people were coming to Gaspra. On December 30 Tolstoy hosted a group of men he later described to Sonya. She duly chronicled their visit: "three revolutionary workers filled with hatred for the rich and dissatisfaction with the present social arrangements, then six sectarians who have lapsed from the Church, three of whom are true Christians, in that they lead a moral life and love their neighbor...There was also an old man, better off and more intelligent than the rest, who apparently wants to go to the Caucasus and found a monastery by the seashore based on new principles. He wants all the brothers to be highly educated, so that this monastery could be a sort of center of learning and civilization; furthermore, the monks would work the land and support themselves through their own labor. A difficult venture but a worthy one."

Tolstoy finally finished his article "On Religion" in 1902. Sonya had been skeptical of his ruminations on the subject for years, but she had learned not to discuss it with him in depth. At the end of 1901, ever loyal, she took up the copying of his works in progress.

DIARY ENTRY (SONYA) **December 1901**

...I have copied out the first chapter of 'On Religion,' and so far I don't particularly like it. He says little that is new, and it seems somewhat insubstantial. We shall see how it goes on! I did not at all like the way L. N. compared people's abandoned faith in religion with an outworn appendix.

She had already explained her own feelings about religion fairly explicitly.

DIARY ENTRY **4 February 1899**

...I don't understand religious discussions: They destroy my own lofty relations with God, which cannot be put into words. There is no precise definition of eternity, infinity, and the afterlife—there are no words for these things, just as there are no words to express my attitudes about the abstract, indefinable, infinite deity and my eternal life in God. But I have no objection to the Church, with its ceremonies and its icons; I have lived amongst these things since I was a child, when my soul was first drawn to God, and I love attending mass and fasting, and I love the little icon of Iversk mother of God hanging over my bed....

LEV TOLSTOY WITH DAUGHTER SASHA AT THE SHORE, SHUVALOV DACHA, MYSKHOR, ALUPKA, CRIMEA, SEPTEMBER/OCTOBER 1901

LEV AND SONYA TOLSTOY, ALUPKA, CRIMEA, 1901

DAUGHTER-IN-LAW OLGA ON STEPS OF VORONTSOV PALACE, ALUPKA, CRIMEA, AUTUMN 1901

SONYA WITH RELATIVES AND FRIENDS, CANYON OF ORYANDA, CRIMEA, DECEMBER 1901

YALTA, CRIMEA, 1902

WEEKS IN GASPRA TURNED into months, Lev and Sonya grew accustomed to the place and missed Yasnaya Polyana less than they had at the beginning. Sonya photographed her guests enjoying the landscapes, the sea, the palace, and the port at Yalta. Lev remained intellectually opposed to the opulence that surrounded him and spent his waking hours preoccupied with his health, his work, and his philosophical thoughts. But even he fell under the spell of their Crimean sanctuary, writing to his brother Sergei, "I live here in a luxurious palace the like of which I have never lived in: wonderful fountains, irrigated lawns in the park, marble staircases, and suchlike. And on top of this is the wonderful beauty of the sea and the mountains."

The family suffered through several cycles in which Tolstoy's health plummeted precipitously, then rebounded.

DIARY ENTRY **22 July 1901**

Lev Nikolaevich is on the mend now. He is taking long walks through the forest and eating and sleeping well. Thank God!...Yesterday when L. N. said that decency demanded that he should die when next he falls ill, I replied: 'Yes, life is depressing when one is old. I too would like to die soon.' At this he suddenly came to life and burst out with passionate indignation: 'No, one must live! Life is beautiful!' It's wonderful to have this energy at the age of 73, and it's this that will save both of us...

Finally, on June 25, 1902, the family left Gaspra. After two days' travel they were back in Yasnaya Polyana.

DIARY ENTRY **26 June 1902**

Yesterday's steamer trip (the first in my life) was beautiful and comfortable. We are now in the train, traveling in a special luxurious carriage fitted with a saloon... Tomorrow we will be home, thank God. L. N.'s stomach and legs ache and we have applied compresses. It's hard to write as the train is jolting....My diary for the Crimea is a special notebook. I am now resuming my old book, and my old life. I thank God that He has granted us to take Lev Nikolaevich home once more! I pray he never has to leave again!

SIX MONTHS AFTER VANECHKA'S DEATH, AUGUST 1895

Marriage

"I was lying in bed today wondering why a husband and wife so often find a certain estrangement creeping into their relations, and why relations with outsiders are often so much more pleasant. And I realized that this is because married couples know every single aspect of one another, both the good and the bad. And as one grows older, one becomes wiser and sees everything more clearly. We do not like people to see our bad side, we carefully conceal our bad traits from others and show ourselves off to our best advantage.... With a husband or wife, though, this is not possible, for everything is so transparently visible. One can see all the lies and all the masks—and it's not at all pleasant." **22 May 1902**

33RD WEDDING ANNIVERSARY, YASNAYA POLYANA, SEPTEMBER 23, 1895

AFTER FORTY-EIGHT YEARS of marriage, at the age of 82, Lev Tolstoy snuck out of the house in the middle of the night, leaving Sonya forever. Sasha, his youngest daughter, helped him pack. Before leaving he wrote Sonya a letter.

October 28, 1910, 4:00 a.m.

My departure will grieve you. I am sorry for that, but please understand and believe that I could not act otherwise. My position in the house is becoming and has become unbearable. Apart from everything else, I can no longer live in these conditions of luxury in which I have been living, and I am doing what old men of my age commonly do: leaving this worldly life in order to live out my last days in peace and solitude.

Please try to understand and do not follow me if you learn where I am. Your coming would only make your position and mine worse and would not alter my decision. I thank you for your honorable forty-eight years of life with me, and I beg you to forgive me for anything in which I have been at fault toward you, as I with all my soul forgive you for any wrong you have done me. I advise you to reconcile yourself with the new position in which my departure places you and not to have an unkindly feeling toward me. If you want to report anything to me, give it to Sasha. She will know where I am and will send on what is necessary; but she can't tell you where I am for I have made her promise not to tell anyone.

Why did Tolstoy decide to sneak out? And why, in light of the fact that Lev and Sonya's marriage has been labeled one of the worst in history, did the couple stay together so long? Divorce was an option in Tolstoy's day. In fact Lev's own sister, Maria, divorced her husband in the summer of 1857 because of his infidelities.

At first Sonya and Lev Tolstoy were most definitely in love. They quarreled soon after their wedding day, but in the beginning their disagreements were trivial. They wanted almost all the same things in life—children, a home brimming with family and friends, days filled with intellectual and spiritual pursuits. Sonya revered Lev's talent and wanted to help him in his work. They drew closer to each other the same time they were beginning to grow apart.

Sonya devoted her energy, intelligence, and capacity for love to her husband and their children and to managing the house. Lev, for his part, depended on her attentions and respected her perceptive criticisms of his literary work. Though he was restless, he enjoyed many aspects of his upper-class life in those early years, including hunting and good company. He devoted himself to literature, concerned himself with managing his lands humanely, and was attached to the children.

Both Tolstoys held strong beliefs that they were continually reexamining. As the years passed, Tolstoy's views veered away from Sonya's. Their differences about politics, religion, and how to conduct family affairs began to wear them both down, and Tolstoy's devotion to the followers who flocked to see him divided them further. But even when Sonya couldn't understand Lev's affection for the peasants, couldn't tolerate his desire to give away his possessions, couldn't accept his repudiation of the Orthodox Church, and was offended by his blasphemy, she stood up for him. They needed each other.

She was exhausted from childbirth, from all the responsibilities she took upon herself, and from the adversity in the house. She was subject to depression and toyed with suicide. In a single diary entry she registered her desire to end it all, alongside her dutiful attentiveness to meal preparation; Tolstoy had become a vegetarian and she catered to his changed dietary wishes, though not without vociferous complaining.

DIARY ENTRY **21 June 1897**

I am not well: when I arrived here [Grumond, a nearby village] I felt something in me had broken, and I still feel this. The strangest sensations are lurking inside me—as though I were just waiting for a pretext to take my life. It has been ripening within me for some time now, and I fear it as I fear madness. Yet I love it too, even though superstition and simple religion cry out against it. I know it's a sin, and I'm afraid of killing myself, for then I would deprive myself of communion with God, and thus with the angels' souls and thus with Vanechka. So as I was walking along today, I fell to thinking how I would write hundreds of letters, which I would send out to everyone I could think of, including the most unlikely people, and in these letters I would explain why I had killed myself. When I actually began to think what I would say in this confession of mine, I found it so touching that I all but wept for myself...I am now terrified of going mad....

And now I have to write out the menu for dinner: soupe printaniére*—oh, how I've grown to loathe* soupe printaniére. *For 35 years, day in day out, it's been* soupe printaniére*...I don't want to have to write* soupe printaniére *ever again, I want to listen to the most difficult fugue or symphony, I want every day to listen to the most complicated musical harmonies and to strive with all my soul to understand the composer's own private, complicated musical language, and what he experienced in the depths of his being when he was composing these works...*

Tolstoy grew increasingly cold, intolerant, and hostile to Sonya's conventional and conservative beliefs. She grew ever more short-tempered, sharp-tongued, and moody. Over the years their relationship went from troubled to tormented. They lived out their marriage as they did everything else—in public, on a grand scale—while in private they recorded their arguments and complaints day-by-day, year-by-year, in their diaries for posterity. Their diaries expose the close intertwining of their hate and love.

Each September 23rd, on their wedding anniversary, Sonya brought out her fine clothes and got dressed up. Whenever she could she celebrated the occasion with a photograph, arranging a scene and stepping into the composition so she and her husband could stand side-by-side.

34TH WEDDING ANNIVERSARY, YASNAYA POLYANA, SEPTEMBER 23, 1896

37TH WEDDING ANNIVERSARY, YASNAYA POLYANA, SEPTEMBER 23, 1899

LEV TOLSTOY'S 75TH BIRTHDAY, YASNAYA POLYANA, AUGUST 1903

DIARY ENTRY (LEV) **14 July 1884**

Missed several days and tried to write everything down from memory on Wednesday. On that day, I think, I asked my wife to come, and she refused with cold spitefulness and the desire to hurt me. I couldn't sleep all night. And during the night I got ready to go away, packed up my things and went to wake her up. I don't know what was the matter with me—bitterness, lust, moral exhaustion—but I suffered terribly.

She got up, and I told her everything, told her that she had ceased to be my wife. A helpmate for her husband? She hasn't helped me for a long time, but only hinders me. A mother to my children? She doesn't want to be. A nurse? She doesn't want to be. A companion of my nights? She makes a bait and a plaything even of that.

I was terribly depressed, and I felt I had spoken uselessly and feebly. I was wrong not to go away. I think I shan't be able to avoid it. I'm terribly sorry for the children, though. I love them more and more and pity them.

DIARY ENTRY (LEV) **9 August 1884**

Came home. Sonya and I were reconciled. How glad I was. Actually if she were to take it upon herself to be good, she would be very good.

DIARY ENTRY (SONYA) **25 October 1886**

...Although the last two months, when Lev Nikolaevich was ill, were an agonizing time for me, strangely enough they were also a very happy time for me. I nursed him day and night and what I had to do was so natural, so simple. It is really the only thing I can do well—making a personal sacrifice for the man I love. The harder the work, the happier I was. Now that he is on his feet again and almost well, he has given me to understand that he no longer needs me. So on the one hand I have been discarded like a useless object, and on the other, impossible, undefined sacrifices are, as always, demanded of me, in my life and in my family, and I am expected to renounce everything, all my property, all my beliefs, the education and well being of my children—things which not only I, a fairly determined woman, but thousands of others who believe in these precepts, are incapable of doing...

DIARY ENTRY (SONYA) **2 October 1897**

Lyovochka invited me out for a game of shuttlecock this evening for some exercise, but I asked him to play a duet with me instead. We played a Beethoven septet quite nicely, and I was in such high spirits afterwards! We went to bed late and I read Menshikov's article 'On Sexual Love' in The Week. This matter will never be settled, however much they may talk about it.

DIARY ENTRY (SONYA) **27 June 1898**

I was astounded today by something L. N. wrote in his notebook concerning women: 'If a woman is not a Christian she is a wild animal.' That means that throughout my life I have sacrificed all my personal life to him and suppressed all my own desires—even a visit to my son, like today—and all my husband can see is animal behavior. The real animals are those men who through their own egotism completely consume the lives of their wives, children, friends—everyone who crosses their path.

(Tolstoy's actual words were: 'A woman can only be liberated if she is a Christian. A liberated woman who is not a Christian is a wild beast.')

DIARY ENTRY (SONYA) **7 September 1908**

It is a very long time since I have written in my diary. I have come in my old age to where two paths lie before me: I can either raise myself spiritually and strive for self-perfection, or I can seek pleasure in food, peace and quiet, and various pleasures like music, books, and the company of others. This last frightens me. My life is set in such a narrow frame; it is a constant effort looking after Lev Nikolaevich, whose health is becoming visibly weaker. When he gets worse I am horrified by the prospect of my pointless empty life without him. When he gets better I feel as though I must prepare myself for this, and assure myself that I shall then be free to serve him—to which end I am presently putting all his manuscripts in order and copying out all his diaries, notebooks, and everything else relating to his creative work.

40TH WEDDING ANNIVERSARY, YASNAYA POLYANA, SEPTEMBER 23, 1902

43RD WEDDING ANNIVERSARY, YASNAYA POLYANA, SEPTEMBER 23, 1905

45TH WEDDING ANNIVERSARY, YASNAYA POLYANA, SEPTEMBER 23, 1907

BOTH TOLSTOYS WERE DEVOTED parents. Their household, which was filled with games, culture, and educational activities, was to a large degree centered on the children. The children loved both parents and were dominated by both of them, but the three girls fell under their father's spell more readily than the boys did. When daughter Tanya was an adult in her early thirties, she wrote down her view of her parents' relationship.

2 August 1896

I am copying some of Papa's old letters to people abroad, and feeling very moved by his profound thoughts, often enough expressed naively, through insufficient knowledge of English, and with spelling mistakes. Some are in Mamma's tiny hand, others corrected by her. What a strange combination, those two! It is rarely one could find two people so different, yet at the same time so profoundly attached to one another. In her very best moments, when she wants to follow him and strives to express his thoughts and views, one is amazed how little Mamma understands him, and how far her conception of his views is from reality. In my bad moments I get angry with her about it, but that is cruel and senseless.

In a memoir completed near the end of his life, in 1933, son Ilya recalled his mother's predicament a half century before when she was 35 and he a boy of 13. The year was 1879. By then Sonya had given birth to ten children, three had died. *But what my mother must have gone through at that time! She loved him with all her being. And she was almost his creation. Out of the fine soft clay that was the eighteen-year-old Sonya Behrs, he had modeled the wife he wanted, and she gave herself to him wholly, lived only for him. And now she saw him suffering, and her interests, which had been their common interests, no longer concerned him. He began to deprecate them and to chafe at their life together. Eventually he even frightened her with threats of a separation, a complete break, and she had a huge complex family on her hands—from Tatyana and Seryozha, who were seventeen and eighteen, to an infant in arms. What was she to do? Could she have followed him then, disposing of all the property as he wished and condemning her children to hunger and want?*

After Tolstoy finished writing *Anna Karenina*, in 1877, his habitual spiritual search and inward scrutiny of personal principles grew particularly intense. As he had many times before, he grappled with and felt ashamed of his sexual appetite. His dependence upon Sonya for its gratification mortified him.

In his 1889 novel, *The Kreutzer Sonata*, he portrayed husband and wife as prisoners of a love-hate relationship they couldn't extricate themselves from. The protagonist in the story, Pozdnyshev, kills his wife in a fit of jealousy, miserably regrets his addiction to sex, and finally repudiates marriage and its preoccupations. Sonya reeled from this expression of Tolstoy's inner turmoil. Tanya, the most diplomatic of the Tolstoy daughters and the most even-handed in her affections toward both her parents, wrote at age 25 how *The Kreutzer Sonata* affected her.

18 October 1889

I am so sad, so depressed, I cannot restrain the tears. That is stupid and not worthy of me; but I feel lost, unhappy, and lonely. I do not know what will come of me or what I ought to do. I have only just decided—since the inception of The Kreutzer Sonata—and decided firmly, not to get married; it used to seem easy and desirable, but now it's all a tangle; my will is shaken, i.e. I cannot dream of remaining single and ought not to think about the opposite.

послѣдній свадебный день
23 Сентября 1910 года.

"THE LAST WEDDING ANNIVERSARY, 23 SEPTEMBER, 1910"

"23 SEPTEMBER, 1910, THERE IS NO HOLDING HIM!"

SEPTEMBER 23, 1910: THE LAST WEDDING ANNIVERSARY—48 YEARS OF MARRIAGE PHOTOGRAPHS BY TOLSTOY'S SECRETARY, VALENTIN BULGAKOV, MADE AT SONYA'S REQUEST (BOTH)

LEV TOLSTOY'S GRAVE, YASNAYA POLYANA, 1911

SONYA HATED TOLSTOY'S faithful follower Vladimir Chertkov. He was cold, calculating, and did everything in his power to undermine the Tolstoys' already difficult marriage. Tolstoy and Chertkov had become inseparable, and this heightened Sonya's suspicions that they were plotting against her. She feared, specifically, that Chertkov would engineer an agreement with Tolstoy that would deprive her of control over her husband's diaries and literary work, the family's future income and his legacy. Her paranoia, her suffering, and her associated hysterical behavior made life in the house intolerable.

Her suspicions were not unfounded. One July day in 1910, Chertkov, Lev Tolstoy, his youngest daughter Sasha, and three others secretly met in a wooded area on the outskirts of the village of Grumond, and Tolstoy signed a revised will that placed all his literary works in the public domain. As for the diaries, they had been in Chertkov's possession for some time already and Sonya managed to repossess them, but not before selected passages had been copied.

Sonya didn't know about the Grumond meeting, but she suspected the worst. On October 27, 1910, in the middle of the night, she woke up gripped with an obsession to find Tolstoy's latest will. She crept into his study, lit a lamp, and proceeded to search through his belongings. Tolstoy, sleeping in the next room, was awakened by the light, her footsteps, and the rustling of paper. Upset profoundly, he made his decision to leave.

He woke Sasha and his doctor, Dushan Makovitsky, whom he told to pack a few medical necessities. At dawn on October 28th, the coachman was summoned to harness the horses and to drive Tolstoy and Makovitsky to the Yasenki railway station. From there the two men traveled south to the only place Tolstoy could think of going, his sister's monastery in the province of Kaluga. But once there he was too much on edge to stay for long. Fearing pursuit, he and Makovitsky, now joined by Sasha, boarded a train with the intention of taking a circuitous route to the Caucasus.

By the time they reached the third transfer point, the Astapovo railroad station, Tolstoy was gravely ill. He was taken off the train and put to bed in the stationmaster's house. Sonya arrived at Astapovo by train on November 3rd. Tolstoy was unconscious when she finally was allowed in to see him. At dawn on November 7, 1910, he died.

Sonya was overcome with grief and remorse, tortured with the idea that she was responsible for her husband's death, repentant about not supporting his ideas. She was bedridden with anguish for weeks, and when she gradually resumed her activities she had lost much of her indomitable energy and no longer showed signs of her former hysteria.

Often she visited Tolstoy's gravesite and photographed it. She continued to work, organizing Tolstoy's books and papers, writing articles, maintaining the house, spending time with her grandchildren, and hosting visitors who continued to arrive.

SELF-PORTRAIT AT TOLSTOY'S GRAVE, YASNAYA POLYANA, 1912

SELF-PORTRAIT, YASNAYA POLYANA, 1910

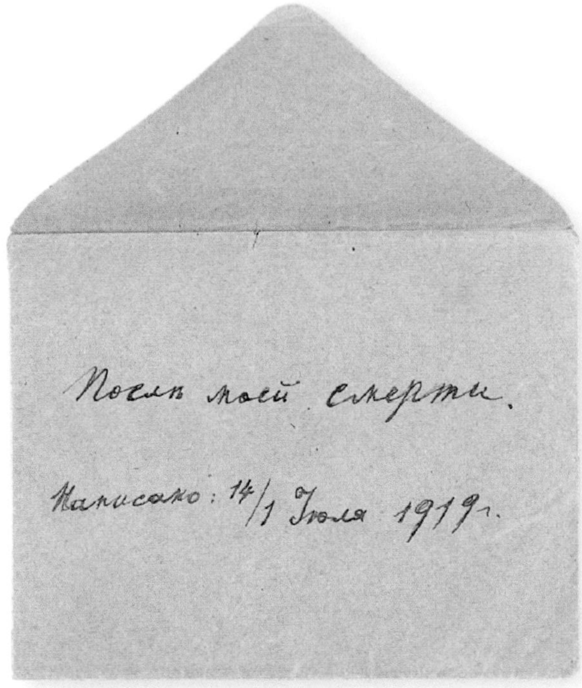

"TO BE OPENED AFTER MY DEATH, 14/1 JULY, 1919"

AFTER TOLSTOY DIED Sonya lived another nine years. She saw the outbreak of World War I, the Russian Revolution of 1917, and the civil war that followed. The Bolsheviks allowed her to remain in Yasnaya Polyana during those years, and her needs were taken care of. She continued to keep a record of domestic occasions and events unfolding in her neighborhood.

DIARY ENTRY **14 July 1919**

...Unrest in Tula; people have been marching with white flags and putting them up over the post-office building. What will come of it? The artist Yuon paid me a visit and praised my flower drawings. I wrote a letter to be opened after my death, bidding farewell to my family and begging forgiveness from those I am abandoning....

She folded the letter and wrote on the envelope, "To be opened after my death." She dated it "14/1 July 1919," referring to both the Julian calendar, used in Russia before 1900, and the Gregorian calendar, 13 days ahead of it. The letter reads:

The circle of my life is closing, I am slowly dying, and to all those with whom I have lived, recently and in the past, I want to say farewell and forgive me.

Farewell my dear children whom I love so much, especially my daughter Tanya, whom I love more than anyone else on earth—I beg her to forgive me for all the pain I have caused her.

Sasha too—forgive me for not giving you enough love, and thank you for your kindness to me in recent days.

Forgive me, sister Tanya, for being unable, despite my unchanging love for you, to comfort you and make things a little easier for you when your life was so lonely and hard. I beg Kolya to forgive me for being unkind to him occasionally. Whatever may have

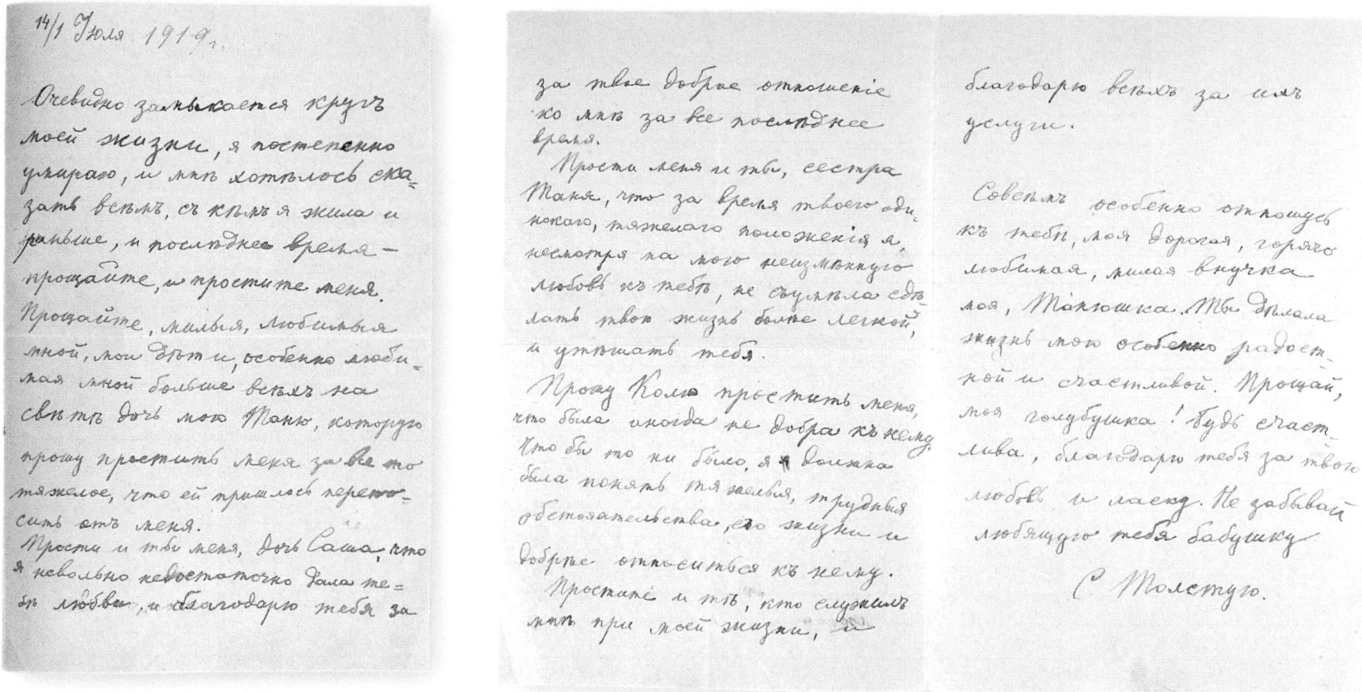

14/1 Іюля 1919 г.

Очевидно замыкается кругъ моей жизни, я постепенно умираю, и мнѣ хотѣлось сказать всѣмъ, съ кѣмъ я жила и раньше, и послѣднее время — прощайте, и простите меня.

Прощайте, милые, любимые мной, мои дѣти и, особенно любимая мной больше всѣхъ на свѣтѣ дочь моя Таню, которую прошу простить меня за все то тяжелое, что ей пришлось перенесть отъ меня.

Прости и ты меня, дочь Саша, что я невольно недостаточно дала тебѣ любви, и благодарю тебя за за твое доброе отношеніе ко мнѣ за все послѣднее время.

Прости меня и ты, сестра Таня, что за время твоего одинокаго, тяжелаго положенія я, несмотря на мою неизмѣнную любовь къ тебѣ, не съумѣла сдѣлать твою жизнь болѣе легкой, и утѣшать тебя.

Прошу Колю простить меня, что была иногда не добра къ нему. Что бы то ни было, я должна была понять тяжелыя, трудныя обстоятельства его жизни и добрѣе относиться къ нему.

Простите и вы, кто служилъ мнѣ при моей жизни, и благодарю всѣхъ за ихъ услуги.

Совсѣмъ особенно отношусь къ тебѣ, моя дорогая, горячо любимая, милая внучка моя, Танюшка. Ты дѣлала жизнь мою особенно радостной и счастливой. Прощай, моя голубушка! Будь счастлива, благодарю тебя за твою любовь и ласку. Не забывай любящую тебя бабушку

С. Толстую.

FINAL LETTER TO FAMILY

happened, I should have realized how difficult his life was and have been more charitable towards him. Forgive me, all you who have served me throughout my life, and thank you for your services. And for you, my precious, dearly beloved granddaughter Tanyushka, I have very special feelings. You have made my life so happy. Farewell, my dove! Be happy, I thank you for all your love and tenderness towards me. Do not forget your granny, who loves you so much,

S. Tolstaya.

DIARY ENTRY **15 July 1919**

I felt so unwell these past few days that I thought my death was near. So I summoned my two darling Tanyas, who have been living with me for three years, and the three of us went through my few valuable possessions together. I considered it only fair to give my best things to my daughter and granddaughter. They have lived with me through the most difficult time in my life and have always been such a comfort to me. To my granddaughter I gave my gold watch and chain, which Lev Nik. gave me, and a large diamond brooch which was a present from him when we were engaged to be married; to my daughter I gave my mother's bracelet (gold) and a ring with two diamonds and a ruby, a present from Lev Nik. for all my help and labors when he was writing Anna Karenina. (This ring was in fact called Anna Karenina.)

Sonya's exceptional strength dwindled gradually. She kept up her diary until October 19, 1919, just 16 days before her death. Her final entries reflect her clear mind, her subdued but still unshakable spirit, and her attentiveness to the world around her. She died in her bed at Yasnaya Polyana from pneumonia on November 4, 1919, at the age of 75.

Technique

Sonya's Tools & Methods

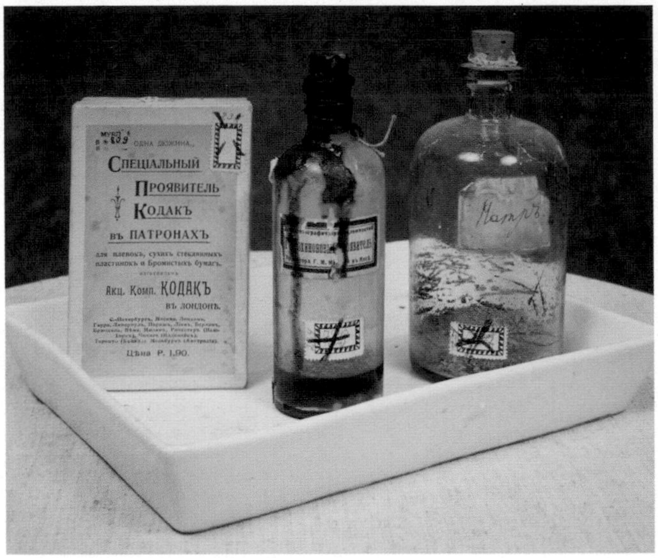

SONYA'S PHOTOGRAPHIC CHEMICALS

A QUARTER CENTURY AND 12 children after Sonya, at age 16, dabbled in photography for a summer she returned to taking pictures. By that time the wet-plate collodion process for sensitizing glass and paper that she had used as a girl had been replaced by the simpler, gelatin dry-plate method. She had to learn photography all over again.

In 1887 her son Sergei helped her purchase a large, portable Kodak camera and worked with her to master it. She carried the camera and the necessary 13 by 18 cm. glass plates around with her in a special road basket. She liked the results she was getting and stayed with the heavy equipment even when a lighter film camera became available at the end of the century.

When she needed further technical advice, she turned to an acquaintance, Albert Mey, owner of a prominent Moscow photography firm, Scherer, Nabgoltz and Company. Occasionally she sent Mey her glass plates for development, but most often she developed them herself in a dark pantry under an attic staircase in the family house at Yasnaya Polyana.

Sonya threw herself into both the aesthetic and technical aspects of her photographic enterprise, learning from visiting photographers whose work she facilitated, sharing her field experiences with family and friends, and attending lectures to keep up with developments in this still-new field. It isn't surprising that Sonya was so eager to embrace the possibilities of photography—it was in her nature to be enthusiastic about new projects, and photography was a perfect way to document the Tolstoys' way of life for posterity, a great ambition of hers. Her granddaughter Anna remembered her rushing around in a loose calico apron, fingernails black from the chemical photographic fixer.

Sonya made contact prints and didn't retouch them. She was able to print on the terrace outside the Yasnaya Polyana house because the paper she used wasn't particularly sensitive to light. When the fixing and washing were finished, Sonya would stick the wet prints onto a window. They fell off when they were dry. The paper gave the prints a brownish hue.

Sonya had no facilities for developing her negatives or making prints in Moscow where the family spent winters for the sake of the children's education. She rarely photographed there because of this, and also because of winter's low light. Both Tolstoy houses—the one in Yasnaya Polyana and the one in Moscow—were without electricity, and Sonya never used supplementary light sources.

Sonya made a total of about a thousand pictures. After Tolstoy's death she selected her favorites and prepared two albums in his memory.

KODAK CAMERA AND 13 BY 18 CM. GLASS PLATES

SONYA AND LEV TOLSTOY ON HIS 75TH BIRTHDAY, AUGUST 28, 1903

The Lives and Times of Sonya and Lev Tolstoy
A Chronology

1828 Lev Nikolaevich Tolstoy is born August 28th

1830 Tolstoy's mother dies

1837 Tolstoy's father dies

1844 Sophia Andreyevna Behrs is born on August 22nd

1862 Lev Tolstoy and Sophia Behrs are married in Moscow and settle down in Tolstoy's estate, Yasnaya Polyana, 100 kilometers (about 62 miles) to the south

Fyodor Dostoyevsky writes House of the Dead

1863 Son Sergei is born on June 23rd

Tolstoy begins *War and Peace*

1864 Daughter Tatyana is born on October 4th

Karl Marx's First International is formed in London

Dostoyevsky's Notes from the Underground is published

1865 First part of *War and Peace* is published in July

1865 (CONT.) Second part of *War and Peace* is published in November

Dostoyevsky's Crime and Punishment is published

1866 Son Ilya is born May 22nd

Dmitri Karakozov attempts to assassinate the Tsar; he is publicly hanged and hundreds are arrested

1867 First three volumes of *War and Peace* are published and work on the book continues

A Polish émigré tries to kill the Tsar in Paris

Populists move into peasant villages to help reform terrible conditions

Ivan Turgenev's Smoke is published

1868 Family travels to Moscow to be with Sonya's father who is dying

1869 Son Lev is born on May 20th

Tolstoy finishes *War and Peace*; the sixth and final volume is published December 4th

Social unrest and political protest grow around the country

1869 (CONT.) Dostoyevsky's *The Idiot* is published

1870 Sonya writes Russian and French grammars for her children; she writes a short story titled *Sparrows*

Tolstoy starts a novel about Peter the Great (which he never finishes); he learns Greek; he prepares simple readers for the peasants

Lenin (Vladimir Ilyich Ulyanov) is born

1871 Daughter Maria is born on February 12th

Tolstoy goes to Samara in central Russia for a health cure and buys a 67,000 acre estate

1872 Son Pyotr is born on June 13th

Tolstoy opens a school for peasant children, then closes it; he is disillusioned and haunted by death

1873 Son Pyotr dies from croup on November 9th

Tolstoy begins work on *Anna Karenina*

The family visits the new estate in Samara

Ilya Repin paints The Volga Barge Haulers

1874 Son Nikolai is born on April 22nd

Russian women students returning from abroad form a secret revolutionary society; they are found out and arrested

Modest Musorgsky composes Pictures at an Exhibition

1875 Son Nikolai dies from meningitis on February 2nd

1875 (CONT.) Daughter Varvara is born and dies immediately on November 1st

The "Russian Herald" publishes chapters 1-14 of *Anna Karenina*

The Union of South Russian Workers, the first working-class organization in the country, supports strikes in Odessa

1876 Sonya begins work on a biography of Tolstoy

Tolstoy continues work on *Anna Karenina*, visits Samara to buy horses for a stud farm he is planning, and begins strict observance of Orthodox rituals

Ivan Turgenev's Virgin Soil is published

1877 Son Andrei is born on December 6th

The "Russian Herald" publishes the final chapters of *Anna Karenina*

Russia declares war on Turkey

1878 Sonya gives up on her biography of Tolstoy
Tolstoy buys more land in Samara; he begins work on a novel about the Decembrist uprising, which he later abandons

Russia signs peace agreement with Turkey

1879 Son Mikhail is born on December 20th

Tolstoy stops working on Decembrists and writes two articles: *What I Believe* and *An Investigation of Dogmatic Theology*

Stalin is born

1880 Fourth edition of the *Works of L.N. Tolstoy* (in eleven volumes) is published

1880 (CONT.) Dostoyevsky's The Brothers Karamazov is published

1881 Son Alexei is born on October 31st

Tolstoy gives up hunting and smoking

Dostoyevsky dies

Tsar Alexander II is assassinated, five assassins are hanged, a repressive regime is put in place; pogroms follow

1882 Tolstoys buy a house in Moscow (Khamovniki)

Tolstoy begins writing, What Then Must We Do?, studies Hebrew, threatens to leave home

New laws forbid Jews to settle in rural areas

Child labor laws are enacted and ignored, censorship on press is strengthened; there are riots at universities in St. Petersburg and Kazan

1883 Tolstoy signs over to Sonya power of attorney to conduct all business concerning their property; he writes What I Believe

Vladimir Chertkov visits Tolstoy for the first time

Alexander III coronation takes place in Moscow

1884 Daughter Sasha is born on June 18th

Tolstoy finishes What I Believe, it is seized by the censor; he begins making his own boots, chopping wood, and drawing water

1885 Sonya unsuccessfully petitions the Empress to be allowed to publish Tolstoy's banned works; she converts a shed on the Moscow property

1885 (CONT.) into a publishing house Tolstoy gives up alcohol and becomes a vegetarian

Chertkov sets up the Intermediary, a competing publishing business to produce cheap books for the masses

1886 Son Alexei dies of quinsy on January 18th

Tolstoy writes The Death of Ivan Ilyich and dictates his play, The Power of Darkness

1887 Sonya takes up photography

Tolstoy writes On Life, The Power of Darkness is published as a pamphlet because staging it is forbidden

Five students, one of them Lenin's brother, are hanged for attempting to assassinate Tsar Alexander III

Tight quotas are set for Jews to enter universities

1888 Son (and last child) Ivan (Vanechka) is born on March 31st

Tolstoy begins writing The Kreutzer Sonata

1889 Tolstoy finishes The Kreutzer Sonata; Sonya hates it, but petitions to get it published

1890 Sonya writes a story, Who Is To Blame, her answer to The Kreutzer Sonata

More repressive laws are passed

Pyotr Tchaikovsky composes The Queen of Spades and The Sleeping Beauty

1891 Tolstoy, denouncing smoking and alcohol, writes Why Do Men Stupefy Themselves?

1891 (CONT.) Tolstoy leads a famine relief effort in the after math of failed harvests; Sonya joins in his work

Construction of Trans-Siberian railway begins

Sergei Rachmaninov composes First Piano Concerto

1892 Sonya rejoins Tolstoy's campaign to alleviate the suffering of famine victims by setting up canteens

1893 Tolstoy's The Kingdom of God is Within You is finished in April, banned by censors, and disseminated anyway

Siberian Rail Company is established and results in migration to Siberia

More restrictions are enacted against the Jews

1894 Sonya produces an edition of Tolstoy's Complete Works

Peasants are denied the right to hold passports

Tsar Alexander III dies, his son Nicholas becomes new Tsar

1895 Son Vanechka dies on February 23rd

Tolstoy works on Resurrection

Master and Man is published

Tolstoy prepares a will in which he leaves his papers to Chertkov and Sonya

Nicholas II authorizes theatrical performance of The Power of Darkness

Nicholas II dismisses representative government as "senseless dreams;" Tolstoy joins in protest;

1895 (CONT.) Marxist movement grows; Lenin and others are arrested, imprisoned, exiled

1896 Tolstoy writes Hadji Murat

Tsar's adviser presses for Tolstoy's imprisonment

Mining and manufacturing growth is rapid; railroads are expanded

Working class grows in number; strikes and arrests spread across Russia

Anton Checkov writes The Seagull and Uncle Vanya

1897 Tolstoy begins writing What is Art?

Russia conducts its first official population census

Another failed harvest is followed by famine

1898 Sonya writes a novella titled Song Without Words

Tolstoy finishes What is Art?

Tolstoy works to help famine victims and supports two persecuted religious sects—the Dukhobors and the Molokans; son Sergei accompanies 2,000 Dukhobors to Canada

The Social Democratic Workers Party is formed

1899 Tolstoy finishes Resurrection; the first part is published in "The Cornfield," proceeds go to the Dukhobors

Students riot at University of St. Petersburg; all universities are closed

Stalin leaves seminary in Georgia and becomes active in revolutionary groups

1900 Sonya accepts position as trustee at Moscow orphanage

Government discusses the prospect of excommunicating Tolstoy

Lenin emerges from Siberian exile and goes abroad

1901 Sonya begins to write her autobiography, My Life

Tolstoy is excommunicated by the Orthodox Church on February 22nd; Sonya protests to no avail

Tolstoy falls ill with malaria; family travels to Crimea for his convalescence

Anton Chechov's Three Sisters is performed for the first time

1902 Tolstoy's health is improved and family returns to Yasnaya Polyana

Tolstoy works on various plays, short stories, and essays

Peasants riot in the countryside; there are assassinations of government officials in St. Petersburg and Kharkov

1903 Radical students and revolutionaries increasingly seek out Tolstoy

On April 6th, Easter, Jews are massacred in Kishinev, Bessarabia; Tolstoy writes to governor of Kishinev to protest

Mensheviks and Bolsheviks split

Trans-Siberian Railway is completed

1904 Sonya writes a short story titled, Groans, under the pseudonym, "A Tired Woman"

1904 (CONT.) *Russia declares war on Japan in January; Port Arthur surrenders to Japan in December*

There is a wave of pogroms in the south and west of Russia

Lenin launches a newspaper

Anton Chekhov dies

1905 Tolstoy writes letters and articles condemning violence

January 9th, Bloody Sunday, begins Russia's first revolution; riots and strikes follow; Tsar forms a consulting assembly, the Duma

In summer there is a general strike in Odessa supported by mutiny on the battleship Potemkin

The Tsar and Empress meet Rasputin for the first time

1906 Sonya falls ill with peritonitis and has surgery

Daughter Maria dies from pneumonia on November 26th

Tolstoy writes On the Significance of the Russian Revolution and starts The Children's Law of God

The First State Duma opens on April 27th and is dissolved on July 9th

1907 Sonya continues work on her autobiography

Sonya's brother is murdered by terrorists; marauders break into Yasnaya Polyana and Sonya appeals to police for help, angering Tolstoy; police seize Tolstoy's books; right wing organization threatens Tolstoy's life; Chertkov returns from exile in England

1907 (CONT.) Tolstoy starts evening class for peasant children, has several strokes and experiences memory losses

Second Duma is dissolved for being too radical

Wassily Kandinsky paints Motley Life

Nikolai Rimsky-Korsakov composes The Legend of the Invisible City of Kitezh

1908 Sonya continues her autobiography

Tolstoy writes *I Cannot Be Silent* appealing to the Tsar for an end to violence; his text is banned but circulates anyway

Tolstoy's 80th birthday is celebrated in September

1909 Tolstoy is ill again

Daughter Sasha and Vladimir Chertkov convince Tolstoy to sign a secret will depriving Sonya of control over his literary estate; Sonya is suspicious and upset

Rachmaninov composes Third Piano Concerto

1910 Tolstoy rewrites his will again; Sonya and he argue violently

Tolstoy leaves home with his doctor and daughter Sasha on October 28th; he dies at Astapovo railway station on November 7th

1911 Sophia, her children, and Chertkov battle over Tolstoy's manuscripts

1913 Daughter Sasha buys Yasnaya Polyana from her mother for 40,000 Rubles; land is transferred to peasants in accordance with Tolstoy's will; Sonya retains the house and orchard and divides the money among her 38 dependents

1914 Legal dispute over Tolstoy's manuscripts is settled in Sonya's favor

Sonya finishes her autobiography

World War I begins; Russia enters on August 2nd

1917 Sonya's daughter Tanya moves to Yasnaya Polyana with her child when her husband dies

Peasants loot and burn estates near Yasnaya Polyana; Sonya applies to Provisional Government for protection and receives it

Tsar abdicates on March 16th Lenin and other exiled revolutionaries return to Russia; Bolsheviks take power in October

1918 *Bolsheviks sign treaty with Germany; civil war begins*

1919 Sonya dies from pneumonia on November 4th

LEV AND SONYA TOLSTOY IN GASPRA, CRIMEA, MAY 1902

A DRY WELL, VILLAGE OF YASNAYA POLYANA, LATE 1890s

Acknowledgments

IN THE YEAR 2000, photographer Sam Abell told me about some photographs he had seen in Russia 17 years earlier, in 1983, while photographing a *National Geographic* magazine story on Leo Tolstoy. "I think there's something there," he said. I thank Sam for those words (which turned out to be consequential for me), and I thank him for his interest in the project ever since.

Three years after Sam's comments, I decided to look into the matter. I wouldn't have gotten very far, however, without the help of colleagues and friends in Russia who had helped me with earlier Russian projects: Nikolai Romanov, Andrei Baskakov, Yuri Rybchinski, and Olga Romanova. Their generosity and advice have a great deal to do with this venture going forward.

Vitaly Remizov, Director of the State Museum of L. N. Tolstoy, Moscow, endorsed the project and gave me permission to enter the museum's rich, wonderful archive and undertake the work. He also made his staff available for support.

During the course of my research I met two women—Marina Loginova in Moscow and Galina Alexeeva at Yasnaya Polyana—who were instrumental in providing me with access to and understanding of Sophia Tolstoy's photography. Marina's expertise and enthusiasm brought a spirit to our work that made the time we spent together enlightening and joyful. Galina was a gracious hostess and guide in Yasnaya Polyana and stepped in with help on logistical questions always at the right moment.

I am extremely grateful to Nina Hoffman, President, and Kevin Mulroy, Publisher of National Geographic Books, for their support and encouragement. I have learned a great deal from both of them and this book has been shaped, in part, by their insights. Art Director Michael Walsh expressed interest in the project from the start, and I am delighted with his thoughtful design.

I also want to extend special thanks to friends, acquaintances, and colleagues who believed in this book of Sophia Tolstoy's work and helped me in big and small ways through several years of ups and downs: Dena Andre, Kathleen Ewing, Becky Lescaze, Diana Walker, Betsy Karel, Philip Brookman, Jane Livingston, Elizabeth Newhouse, Rosemary DeRosa, Alison Kahn, and Mary Nash.

And thank you to my family: Oren Bendavid-Val for an early reading of the text, Beth Bendavid-Val for looking at cover candidates, Ronnit Bendavid-Val for being her optimistic self, Naftali Bendavid and Dara Corrigan Bendavid for being understanding about my lack of availability at times, and Avrom for his patience and support, always.

Song Without Words

The Photographs & Diaries of Countess Sophia Tolstoy

LEAH BENDAVID-VAL

Published by the National Geographic Society
John M. Fahey, Jr., President and Chief Executive Officer
Gilbert M. Grosvenor, Chairman of the Board
Nina D. Hoffman, Executive Vice President;
President, Book Publishing Group

Prepared by the Book Division
Kevin Mulroy, Senior Vice President and Publisher
Leah Bendavid-Val, Director of Photography Publishing and Illustrations
Marianne R. Koszorus, Director of Design

Barbara Brownell Grogan, Executive Editor
Elizabeth Newhouse, Director of Travel Publishing
Carl Mehler, Director of Maps

Staff for This Book
Kevin Mulroy, Project Editor
Rebecca Lescaze, Text Editor
Michael J. Walsh, Art Director
Michael Horenstein, Production Project Manager
Meredith C. Wilcox, Illustrations Specialist
Cameron Zotter, Design Assistant

Jennifer A. Thornton, Managing Editor
Gary Colbert, Production Director

Manufacturing and Quality Management
Christopher A. Liedel, Chief Financial Officer
Phillip L. Schlosser, Vice President
John T. Dunn, Technical Director
Chris Brown, Director
Maryclare Tracy, Manager
Nicole Elliott, Manager

Half-title page: grandson Volodya Tolstoy, February 1903, photo by Sophia Tolstoy

Printed in Italy

Founded in 1888, the National Geographic Society is one of the largest nonprofit scientific and educational organizations in the world. It reaches more than 285 million people worldwide each month through its official journal, NATIONAL GEOGRAPHIC, and its four other magazines; the National Geographic Channel; television documentaries; radio programs; films; books; videos and DVDs; maps; and interactive media. National Geographic has funded more than 8,000 scientific research projects and supports an education program combating geographic illiteracy.

For more information, please call
1-800-NGS LINE (647-5463)
or write to the following address:

National Geographic Society
1145 17th Street N.W.
Washington, D.C. 20036-4688 U.S.A.

Visit us online at www.nationalgeographic.com/books

For information about special discounts for bulk purchases, please contact National Geographic Books Special Sales: ngspecsales@ngs.org

ISBN: 978-1-4262-0173-8

Copyright © 2007 Leah Bendavid-Val
All rights reserved. Reproduction of the whole or any part of the contents without permission is prohibited.

Library of Congress Cataloging-in Publication Data

Tolstaia, S. A. (Sof'ia Andreevna), 1844-1919
Song without words : the photographs and diaries of countess Sophia Tolstoy / Leah Bendavid-Val
p. cm.
ISBN 978-1-4262-0173-8
1. Photography, Artistic. 2. Photography—Russia—History—19th century. 3. Tolstaia, S. A. (Sof'ia Andreevna), 1844-1919. 4. Tolstaia, S. A. (Sof'ia Andreevna), 1844-1919—Diaries.
I. Bendavid-Val, Leah. II. Title.
TR652.T65 2007
779.092—dc22

2007013331

All photos courtesy The State Museum of L. N. Tolstoy, Moscow, unless otherwise noted.

p. 2, Vladimir Smirnov; p. 32, Bibliothèque nationale de France; pp. 34 & 35, State Historical Museum, Moscow; p. 45, Vladimir Smirnov; p. 79, RIA Novosti; p. 144, Digital Image © The Museum of Modern Art/Licensed by SCALA/Art Resource, NY; p. 145 (both), V&A Images; pp. 146 & 147, Digital Image © The Museum of Modern Art/Licensed by SCALA/Art Resource, NY; pp. 160 & 162 (lower), M. Dmitriev/PhotoSoyuz; pp. 162 (upper) & 163, Lobovikov/PhotoSoyuz; p. 171, Vladimir Smirnov; pp. 228 & 229, Vladimir Smirnov.

All diary and letter excerpts courtesy The State Museum of L. N. Tolstoy, Moscow;
English translation from "The Diaries of Sophia Tolstoy" Translated by Cathy Porter, Random House, New York, 1985

Song Without Words: The Photographs and Diaries of Countess Sophia Tolstoy is a traveling exhibition organized by National Geographic in association with the Katzen Arts Center, American University.

the Katzen — American University Museum, College of Arts & Sciences

An exhibition from NATIONAL GEOGRAPHIC

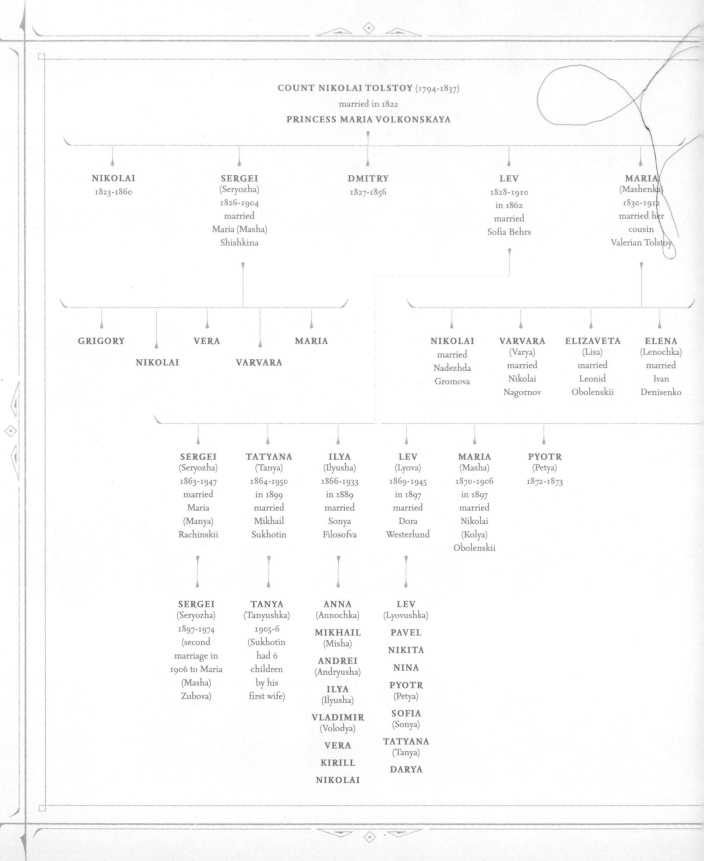

COUNT NIKOLAI TOLSTOY (1794-1837)
married in 1822
PRINCESS MARIA VOLKONSKAYA

- **NIKOLAI** 1823-1860
- **SERGEI** (Seryozha) 1826-1904 married Maria (Masha) Shishkina
  - **GRIGORY**
  - **NIKOLAI**
  - **VERA**
  - **VARVARA**
  - **MARIA**
- **DMITRY** 1827-1856
- **LEV** 1828-1910 in 1862 married Sofia Behrs
  - **SERGEI** (Seryozha) 1863-1947 married Maria (Manya) Rachinskii
    - **SERGEI** (Seryozha) 1897-1974 (second marriage in 1906 to Maria (Masha) Zubova)
  - **TATYANA** (Tanya) 1864-1950 in 1899 married Mikhail Sukhotin
    - **TANYA** (Tanyushka) 1905-6 (Sukhotin had 6 children by his first wife)
  - **ILYA** (Ilyusha) 1866-1933 in 1889 married Sonya Filosofva
    - **ANNA** (Annochka)
    - **MIKHAIL** (Misha)
    - **ANDREI** (Andryusha)
    - **ILYA** (Ilyusha)
    - **VLADIMIR** (Volodya)
    - **VERA**
    - **KIRILL**
    - **NIKOLAI**
  - **LEV** (Lyova) 1869-1945 in 1897 married Dora Westerlund
    - **LEV** (Lyovushka)
    - **PAVEL**
    - **NIKITA**
    - **NINA**
    - **PYOTR** (Petya)
    - **SOFIA** (Sonya)
    - **TATYANA** (Tanya)
    - **DARYA**
  - **MARIA** (Masha) 1870-1906 in 1897 married Nikolai (Kolya) Obolenskii
  - **PYOTR** (Petya) 1872-1873
- **MARIA** (Mashenka) 1830-1912 married her cousin Valerian Tolstoy
  - **NIKOLAI** married Nadezhda Gromova
  - **VARVARA** (Varya) married Nikolai Nagornov
  - **ELIZAVETA** (Lisa) married Leonid Obolenskii
  - **ELENA** (Lenochka) married Ivan Denisenko